"As someone who has personally benefited from Brian's wisdom and friendship, I wholeheartedly endorse *Driving Through Fog*. This transformative book equips readers with simple and proven principles that can serve as guideposts through the often confounding journey of leadership. Brian's emphasis on prioritizing people and selfless service sparked a passion for impacting others and re-discovering the fun of true community. Through expert guidance and personal experience, Brian will help you overcome obstacles, embrace wisdom, and find more joy in collaboration. *Driving Through Fog* is brimming with authentic encouragement, reminding us that choosing hope unlocks the best parts of life. Prepare for a personal and practical journey as Brian's words ignite your spirit, leading you towards a life of impact and clarity through the unavoidable fog of life and leadership."

— **Ted Coniaris, Community Pastor and Expressions Leader**
Community Christian Church

"It is haunting how quickly you can find yourself in the fog. One moment all is well, and the next moment our vision is obscured, our hearts race, and our minds are seized with anxiety and anger. It's easy to lose your bearing, your place, your sense of identity in the fog. As no stranger to the fog, Brian Zehr provides guideposts for navigating complexity and uncertainty while staying true to ourselves, our faith, and our connections. This principle-centered book offers the reader clear and purposeful guidance from decades of experience in navigating and coaching others through their fog. The section on wisdom is a standalone gold mine!"

— **Rev. Jeff Stark, D.Min**

Associate Professor of Theology

Director | Center for Theological Leadership

Olivet Nazarene University

Author of *The News is Good*

Praise for DRIVING THROUGH FOG

"If I only had a dollar for every time I've uttered the words, 'Remember what Brian said?!' I've had the benefit of participating in and reaping the benefits of Brian Zehr's Christ-centered coaching and wisdom for almost twenty years. Brian now brings his leadership experience, wit, and love for the Lord to *Driving Through Fog* – a roadmap of principles designed to help Christian leaders of all types navigate through the challenges of professional and personal life. This is a must-read for any faith-based leader looking to transform their organization, nonprofit, church, community, or home."

— **Ken Brissa, CEO | Phoenix Rescue Mission**

"I have been leading a business for over 20 years, and I recall many times when I have felt like I was in a fog. A fog can make you feel many things or emotions. But for me, the fog often makes me feel bewildered. Brian's book gives me a place to start. Having the guts to take the next step in a fog can be paralyzing. This book gives you the confidence to take that next step. Navigating the fog is something I didn't know how to do. Thanks, Brian, for some practical advice!"

— **Dan Graham, Chairman & CEO | Compass Mortgage**

"A generation ago, Bob Dylan declared: 'The Times They Are A-Changin''. What Dylan prophesied in the 1960s seems truer than ever for leaders in the 21st century. A leader's job is to move forward, even when she can't see what's ahead. Here's a resource to help you do that safely and effectively. My friend and colleague, Brian Zehr, has written an important book based on real-world principles he has learned and developed to help us navigate these challenging times. Brian is a thought leader, a practitioner, and a dear friend who has helped me and the organization I lead keep moving forward despite the fog. This book is an excellent resource if you are trying to move forward and find the fog thick."

— **Patrick O'Connell, Global Director | NewThing**

"In my experience working as an organizational psychologist in a variety of leadership settings, I believe you will benefit from reading and applying this book, *Driving Through Fog*. Brian Zehr is a clear communicator, and many have been impacted by his ability to provoke new thinking. The way Brian explains the principles of navigating the fog we live in to remain healthy through unclear times, rather than promising a cure for the fog, is very helpful. For many years, I've observed Brian modeling these principles and leading his own life in this way. If you want to see a way through your own fog, read this book."

— **Doug McKinley, Psy.D. | Author of *The Resiliency Quest***

Driving Through Fog

Leading Yourself And Others When You Can't See Where You're Going

Brian Zehr

Driving Through Fog © copyright 2023 by Brian Zehr

Published by Streamline Books
www.streamlinebookspublishing.com

All rights reserved.

To protect the privacy of certain individuals within this book, some names and identifying details have been changed.

No part of this book may be reproduced, distributed, or transmitted in any form or by any means, including photocopying, recording, or other electronic or mechanical methods, without the written permission from the author, except in the case of brief quotations embodied in a book review.

Scriptures taken from the Holy Bible, New International Version®, NIV®. Copyright © 1973, 1978, 1984, 2011 by Biblica, Inc.™ Used by permission of Zondervan. All rights reserved worldwide. www.zondervan.com The "NIV" and "New International Version" are trademarks registered in the United States Patent and Trademark Office by Biblica, Inc.™

Cover design by Hannah Crabb | Cover image by wirestock on Freepik
This book was design with images by Zlatko Najdenovski on Flaticon.

ISBN:

979-8-89165-009-1 (paperback)
979-8-89165-010-7 (hardback)
979-8-89165-011-4 (e-book)

July 26th, 2023

To Judy.

There is no one I would rather drive through the fog with.

Contents

Foreword — xiii
by Dave Ferguson

Preface — xix

Introduction — xxiii

1. The Foundation Principle — 1
2. The Priority Principle — 21
3. The Wisdom Principle — 35
4. The Collaboration Principle — 67
5. The Intentionality Principle — 85
6. The Hope Principle — 99

Our Final Destination — 111
Acknowledgments — 119
About the Author — 121
Notes — 123

Foreword
by Dave Ferguson

It was a foggy Sunday when I got to know Brian Zehr.

The fog wasn't hanging in the air, but the fog was hanging over Brian's life.

I knew of Brian, but I didn't really know Brian. He had helped start one of the most exciting and successful churches in Chicagoland. He had garnered a reputation for being a smart strategic leader that both valued people and knew how to mobilize them for action. He had a great reputation.

So, like I said, I knew of Brian. But I didn't know Brian.

That foggy Sunday, I got to know Brian as I drove him to visit multiple locations of the church that I lead. Visiting various locations was my excuse to spend time with Brian and see if I could be of help to him. The fog was thick in his life.

He told me it was hard for him to see what was next for his family. He loved his wife and two kids, but an unwanted fog had settled in, and a future together was starting to seem impossible.

He told me it was hard for him to look back on the church he started and led. While most thought it was a very fruitful ministry, he was now processing those years trying to determine what was healthy and what was unhealthy.

During the next several hours of driving together, I listened to Brian navigate through the dense and unexpected fog of his life.

What I learned about Brian on that foggy Sunday is still true today.

- Brian Zehr relentlessly loves God.
- Brian Zehr is remarkably courageous.
- Brian Zehr will always prioritize growth.
- Brian Zehr is strong and resilient.
- Brian Zehr is a visionary leader.

For the next several years, I got to watch Brian bravely drive through the fog. I got a passenger seat view as I saw Brian's fog fade into the review mirror of the past.

He joined my small group, courageously told them his story, and then asked them to help him maneuver the unforeseen twists and turns that were coming his way.

He met Judy (thanks to my wife's introduction), a remarkable woman who shared his love for life, faith, and the Chicago Cubs! They were clearly meant to be together.

He began to share his story as a way of helping others traverse the hazardous fog that, without warning, rolled into their lives.

I was so impressed with Brian's character that I asked him to join the leadership staff and teaching team at our church.

After watching Brian drive through his own fog, I remember the meeting when he told me he wanted to give driving lessons and help people like you steer through the unpredictable hazards of life. The vision was to start his own company that would provide coaching for people like you. He wanted to write books to help people like you. While the road to get there was blurry and unclear, Brian comfortably settled into the driver's seat and hit the accelerator. And for the last fourteen years, Brian has been helping leaders, churches, and organizations all over the world get clarity when everything around them is foggy.

This book, *Driving Through Fog*, is an immensely helpful rule of the road for life. Yes, it is a book with a lot of answers, but it is more than a book of answers. It is a handwritten map by a person who has been where you are and is willing to journey with you. This book is authored by someone who knows what you are going through. He has felt what you feel, hurt like you hurt, doubted like you doubt, dared to believe like you do, and decided to drive even though the fog is creating hazardous conditions.

Brian's 6 principles of foundation, priority, wisdom, collaboration, intentionality, and hope are signposts to guide you to a new and better tomorrow. I have watched Brian live these principles and they work. I have sat under Brian's teaching of these principles and have personally benefited from them. I have integrated them into my own teaching and seen them positively impact the lives of thousands and thousands of people.

As I am writing this foreword, it is an unexpectedly foggy day in Chicago. Our city's famous skyline is shrouded in smoky clouds. The smoke from the Canadian wildfires, more than one thousand miles away, has taken everyone by surprise. No one saw it coming. The summer days that Chicagoans all live for are suddenly hazardous as the air quality was ranked the worst of any city in the world. And it has disrupted much of life. It is unclear when this haze will lift. Because of these unforeseen conditions, I was forced to drive in the fog.

So, it is in life.

Foreword

You are among the most fortunate, what you are about to read in *Driving Through Fog* will safely get you through the blurry days ahead.

Dave Ferguson
Lead Pastor of Community Christian Church
Author of Hero Maker & B.L.E.S.S.

Preface

As you work through this book, you'll note that, at the beginning of each chapter, I have included "Recommended Listening as You Drive."

The purpose behind this is that music, like many of us, means a lot to my personal journey and how I process thought, emotion, and words. Therefore, the songs you'll see that I added for recommended listening are songs that guide the mood and tone behind each ensuing chapter.

Whether you listen to the recommended song before, during, or after each respective chapter, I hope the lyrics of those songs and their accompanying sound give you an idea of what led to each principle, and maybe even help you think differently about those songs each time you hear them from this point on.

After all, when we find ourselves driving through the murkiness of fog, sometimes it's the music playing through our car speakers that makes us feel a little less alone.

Driving Through Fog

"Do you see anything?"

— Jesus of Nazareth

Introduction

RECOMMENDED LISTENING AS YOU DRIVE:
Waves by Imagine Dragons

I was sitting on the floor in a cold living room—alone. I had just quit my job as a pastor at a church I had been at for almost 17 years. Following a season of growth and success, I had been through so much personal and professional crisis that I was just completely done. I left the job in an unsuccessful attempt to save my marriage. I was utterly alone and in the densest fog I could imagine. When I tried to see what was ahead, I could barely see the rest of the day, much less the next day. I saw nothing.

Have you ever driven a car in a deep fog? A haze in front of you that causes you to squint and grip the steering wheel tightly? You can barely make out the side of the road, the lines, or maybe a car in front of you. There are many different types of fogs in our lives that inhibit us from seeing the road ahead.

Often fog surprises us. We don't see it coming. Surprises are great when you are a child. The older we get, though, the more surprises jolt us into a misty layer of uncertainty. Sometimes fog surprises us with adversity where our lives fall apart like a hundred-car pileup. It might be relationships that deteriorate and leave us unsure of whether we really can move forward. It might be financial or vocational. It shows up in a doctor's diagnosis. Fog may be a recurring depression that leaves us uncertain whether we want to go on.

Other times the fog is a dream that's gone wayward. You thought that life would make sense by now. That you would have figured it out by now. Fog can sometimes result from drifting through the years without intentional living. One day we wake up and find ourselves directionless and lost.

No matter what the fog looks like, "time doesn't hear when we ask it to wait." We still have to and need to move forward.

When we realize that we're in a fog, we tend to enter survival mode. How fast do I drive? What's on the other side of the fog? Should I fly off or freeze?

Alone on the cold living room floor in survival mode. Fog surrounding me. Out of habit I grabbed a Bible and a journal. Those two things became resources to help sort out my emotions and, in many ways, get direction in the journey of life. Little did I realize that this day on the floor I would receive something that would give me hope not just in the moment but for the rest of my life. Memory doesn't serve me well in how I found it, but I opened my Bible and read these hope-filled words:

> "I will lead the blind by ways they
> have not known,
> along unfamiliar paths I will guide
> them;
> I will turn the darkness into light
> before them
> and make the rough places smooth.
> These are the things I will do;
> I will not forsake them."
>
> —Isaiah 42:16

I received it as a promise that I continue to hold onto today. God leads the blind forward into unforeseen and new destinations. He is always with us. What feels rough now will eventually become smooth.

This promise led me to a way of life, a series of principles that, when applied, carve out a path for moving forward when I cannot see where I am going. These principles are key to leading ourselves and others when we do not see the road ahead. I don't believe they clear away the fog, but they help us navigate through the fog.

- <u>Foundation Principle:</u> A foundation is where everything else is built from. We have to look inward to build our foundation. When values, narratives, and behaviors are aligned, we thrive. But often we are not aware of what we value, the stories we tell, or the actions we take.
- <u>Priority Principle:</u> The priority is always people. When it's natural to clam up or close up, it's imperative we choose to serve people. Giving back to others has a way of giving back to us and creating clarity in the fog. Our priority is to focus on others rather than ourselves.
- <u>Wisdom Principle:</u> Overcoming obstacles is about embracing paradoxes and making decisions. Wisdom is indispensable in our navigation through the fog. Without wisdom we can quickly become lost. With wisdom we can go further than we hoped.
- <u>Collaboration Principle:</u> Moving forward together is essential and worth the challenge. Fog can tempt us to take it solo, but it's crucial we travel the path together. We choose to collaborate and

reap the unexpected and unpredictable joys of community.
- <u>Intentionality Principle:</u> Life is best lived on purpose, especially when we cannot see up ahead. Will we wander aimlessly or move in a set direction? The fog gives an amazing opportunity to choose to grow and equip ourselves for what lies ahead. It doesn't happen if we don't do it intentionally.
- <u>Hope Principle:</u> Real change is a process that requires overcoming and learning from adversity. Adversity and suffering will find all of us eventually. We must choose hope if we are to move forward in the fog. Without hope we will sink into darkness. With hope we will find light and life.

Each section of this book will walk through a principle and how to harness its potential for the confusion, discouragement, and inconsistencies you face. You will also find questions at the end of each principle that help you summarize and apply the principles in your own life and context. You'll notice references to scripture or Biblical principles throughout the book. No matter where you place yourself on the faith spectrum, know that you're accepted, and I think you'll find these helpful. I'm not purposefully trying to force Biblical wisdom into this conversation. I can't *not* mention scripture. It's become the bedrock of my life, imagination, and leadership, and it naturally flows through my thoughts.

There's a story about Jesus that never ceases to fascinate me.

In Mark 8 a blind man is brought to Jesus by his friends. They ask Jesus to heal him from his blindness. We don't even know if the blind man believes that Jesus can heal him, but his friends do. And Jesus does the strangest thing. He spits on the blind man's eyes. I can't imagine the man's reaction. Was he used to people spitting in his face? Of course the friends don't understand why Jesus spat on his eyes. And to be honest I'll never understand why he did either. What's the value of putting saliva on someone's eyes? After Jesus spits on his eyes, he touches him and asks him a simple yet life-altering question: "Can you see anything?"

The blind man responds, "I see people, but they look like trees." My first reaction is to question how he knows what trees look like. Maybe he used to be able to see, but now he can't. Maybe he's been blind his whole life and leaned up against a lot of trees. Either way I think Jesus asks us the same question, "Can you see anything?" I'm not sure if he's expecting a yes or no answer, but Jesus is inviting us to join him on a journey of life, leadership, healing, and moving forward even when people look like trees and life is unclear.

I invite you to join this journey with me. Not because I believe I have all the answers or can make your fog go away. But because I believe we can journey together through the uncertainty life inevitably brings using time-tested principles I've seen work for countless others.

Chapter 1
The Foundation Principle

RECOMMENDED LISTENING AS YOU DRIVE:
Silhouettes by Colony House

Finding Direction in the Fog

There is an old story of a Rabbi living in a Russian city. Disappointed by his lack of direction and purpose in his life. He decided to go out into the chilly evening. With his hands thrust deeply into his pockets, he wandered the streets, questioning his faith in God, questioning the scriptures, even questioning his calling to ministry.

The only thing colder than the Russian air was the chill in his soul. He was so discouraged that he wandered into a Russian military compound that was off-limits to civilians.

Into the silence he suddenly heard the harsh

voice of a Russian soldier: "WHO ARE YOU? AND WHAT YOU ARE DOING HERE?"

"Excuse me?" the Rabbi replied.

"Who are you? What are you doing here?"

After a brief moment the Rabbi softly asked the soldier, "How much do you get paid every day?" Taken aback the soldier said, "What does that have to do with anything?"

The Rabbi, suddenly lifted from his discouragement, said, "I will pay you the equal sum if you will ask me those same two questions every day: Who are you? And what are you doing here?"

I want to ask you those two questions. Who are you? What are you doing here? You see, I think we forget. Or we just go through the motions. And in order to move forward we need to remember who we are and where we are. If we don't know the answers to these two questions in the fog, we will inevitably get lost.

Fog creates dangerous driving conditions. It reduces visibility, makes it hard to spot hazards, and it becomes difficult for a driver to judge distance. The dramatic weather conditions can create optical illusions. We don't feel grounded to the road we have been driving on.

Whatever fog we might find ourselves in, within the fog we also find a high level of disruption. Change. The power of this change comes in the form of uprootedness. We can find ourselves disconnected from the life we have been accustomed to living. Think about the most challenging times of your life. You might find yourself in one of them now. Does the ground feel stable? Do you know how to move forward? When our very foundation of life is questioned, we can feel as if we are suddenly in survival mode. Within survival mode, we find ourselves disoriented and unsure of who we are and what we are doing.

For the past decade and a half, the work that I have done with organizations and leaders has dealt with culture, both organizational culture and individuals who build those cultures. The components of this culture build a foundation that grounds us as we move forward. There are three components that must be aligned in order to move forward in any fog: values, narrative, and behaviors.

Let me give you an overview of them before we move into the specifics of how we can build a foundation for driving through fog.

1. Values. Values answer the question, "What is most valuable to me?" Within the disruption of fog, we begin to question what we value. Sometimes our inability to see ahead uproots what we previously prioritized and gives us the amazing opportunity to define and focus on what we value.

While sitting on the living room floor (and in other foggy times of my life), I have found myself reevaluating my values. What is important to me? Not "What *should* be my values?" or "What *were* my values in the past?" but "What *are* they now?" Often people struggle to define their values. They end up with ghost values, what they think their values ought to be instead of what they really are.

2. Narrative. The second component of this foundation is narrative. What is the story I have told myself about who I am and about the life I live? Narratives help us live out our values. Our values become real as we learn ways to articulate them to ourselves and to others. For example, if I say I value helping others but my attitude and words are always critical and self-absorbed, I am going to find myself misaligned and unstable. Narrative must align with values.

3. Behavior. The last component of our foundation is behavior. But it's not just behavior, it's behavioral patterns. What are we doing that supports the values we have with the language and the stories that we tell? We can usually tell a lot about our behavioral patterns by how we spend our money, use our time, and the habits we establish for our daily lives.

What do you value?
What are your narratives?
What are your behavioral patterns?

Let's take a look at each of these components. Each of these is critical on its own because, when combined and aligned, they make the foundation that is essential in moving forward.

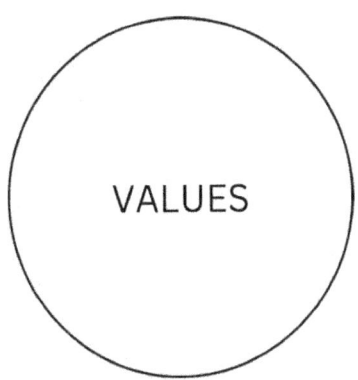

Values

When you define what is most important to you, what is most valuable, you can begin to move forward. Until values are defined, life in the fog remains overwhelming and unstable.

In answering the values question, many resort to what Patrick Lencioni refers to as "permission to play" values.[1] These are values such as honesty, integrity, love, and many other values that everyone would say they have. I've never met anyone who would admit that they value dishonesty or hatred. When asking what your values are, the deeper question is, what is uniquely important to you? What do you believe in that you would give yourself to? It's these values that ground us as we move through the fog.

For example, one of my core values is investing in people. That's not just a "permission to play" value but core to who I am. A question I find myself consistently asking is how do I help people and come alongside them? The starting point is defining the value, and asking how these values work themselves out consistently in our daily lives.

What do you value that will ground you as you move forward?

The temptation when driving through fog is to stand still. It can feel paralyzing, like we cannot move and we lack momentum. The literal definition of momentum is the product of the mass of a particle and its velocity. In other words, the size and speed together moving forward. Figuratively, momentum is more of what moves you forward in light of the things that will hold you back. What moves us forward when we cannot see where we are going?

Dave Ramsey has a formula that he uses to build momentum which I believe we can all find valuable.

$$\frac{\text{Focused Intensity}}{\text{Time}} \times \text{God} = \text{Momentum}$$

Momentum is determined by our focused intensity multiplied by prayer—what he calls the God factor. Ramsey's formula is genius because it forces us to reflect on what we focus on. It also reminds us that prayer and connecting with God is indispensable in building momentum. Thirdly, Ramsey reminds us we can never get past the time factor. In our quick-fix culture we have to remind ourselves that all good things take time, and often take far longer than what we hope.[2]

You can be focused on very few things and focused with intensity on even fewer things. What will you be focused on in order to build momentum? It all starts with values. If we have a lack of focus and lack of connection with God, we will inevitably lose momentum. This is why naming our values is critical to our foundation. If you want to get back up on your feet, if you want to start taking steps through the fog, you have to know what you stand for.

What drives you underneath the surface? What

values make up the essence of who you are? Not just the surface "permission to play" values but the core motivations? If you have a hard time thinking of them, I encourage you to ask your close community what they see in you.

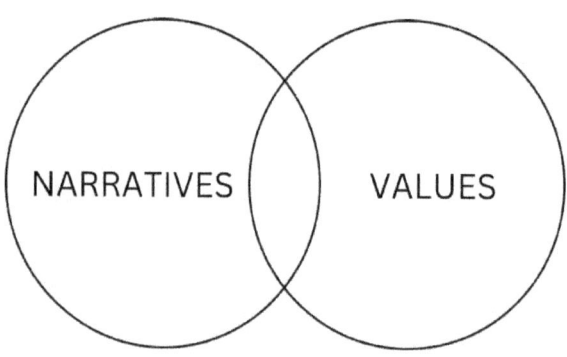

Narratives

The stories we tell and the lives we live either move us forward with integrity or they take us sideways. What is our self-narrative? Have you ever thought about what you think about yourself? The stories we tell about ourselves, others, and the world aren't just fairy tales. They have huge implications for the trajectory of our lives because we live out the stories we believe.

The miracle of LASIK eye surgery changed my narrative from being a person defined by what I can't see to someone who can move forward with confidence.

I was one of those kids who wore glasses at a very early age. There are a lot of pictures of me wearing dark rimmed glasses as a 6-year-old boy. Most of the time, the glasses had duct tape on one or both of the hinges to hold the glasses together. My eyesight was so bad that I would wake up in the morning and not be able to see anything until I put on my glasses. As a 15 year old, I started wearing soft contact lenses, and I would wear them 16+ hours a day. My eyesight was a big part of how I lived my life. It was a narrative that I just accepted. In many ways it was a part of how I defined myself. My story included a deficiency of sight. I could not see without help. It's what I took with me everywhere I went.

Until one day in my mid-thirties, I found the courage (and the money) to have LASIK eye surgery. LASIK stands for Laser-Assisted In Situ Keratomileusis and is a procedure that permanently changes the shape of the cornea, the clear covering of the front of the eye, using an excimer laser. In other words, it is miraculous. I remember having the procedure and needing to wear dark glasses and basically keep my eyes closed for the rest of the day. The next morning I woke up, and for the first time in decades, I could see the alarm clock and everything else with clear, beautiful 20/10 eyesight! How I lived my life changed from that day on. It only took a few days for me to start to take my vision for granted, but I'll never forget how I talked about what I saw, how I moved freely without help, and how everything changed for me.

The narrative in our life is the story we tell about ourselves and what is valuable to us. It comes out in our speech and in the way we see our world. That is true both literally with what our eyes tell us and figuratively with how we live and speak about our values. Our narratives often do not originate with us but are handed down to us from parents, family, role models, or communities. Just like we subconsciously inherit values from our environment, we do the same with narratives.

If you believe the story that you deserve to be in the hard place where you are at, you're incompetent, or you're incomplete in some way, then your chances of driving through the fog will lessen. The stories you believe about the fog when you're in it will determine its power over you. Do you believe you will never get out, or do you believe it will pass? Do you believe you're being punished, or do you believe that it's out of your control?

For me I somehow believed I was less whole because I could not see, and I was able to get surgery to correct my eyesight. The truth is I was always whole and secure no matter if I had 20/10 vision or not. In leading ourselves, we must audit our narratives. While I'll give you helpful suggestions to consider, I should note that the help of a professional counselor or the wise counsel of a friend can be indispensable and sometimes necessary.

What stories do you find yourself repeating in your head? How do these stories affect your emotional health and self-image? Are your narratives creating momentum in your life or dragging you down? How do those stories influence your behavior?

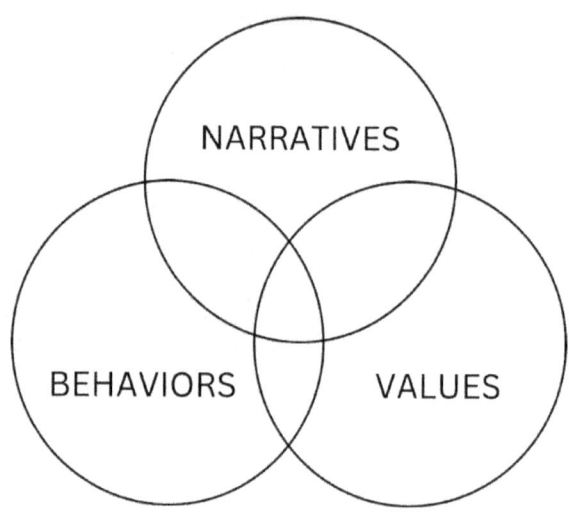

Behaviors

At the end of the day, it's really all about the behavioral patterns that support what we value. Behavior is critical to our foundation.

Whatever we see as valuable and say is important requires behavioral alignment. We need to intentionally take action that aligns with our values and narrative when we cannot see what is ahead. If our actions don't match our values and narrative, then we will be lost, walking in circles.

To say I am a golfer is a little presumptuous, but I play a lot of golf. I think Heaven is full of golf courses. If you don't like golf, Heaven may not be for you.

The Foundation Principle

One winter, three of my friends and I decided to escape the cold of Chicago and take in a few days of golf in Florida. I was in a golf cart with my friend Ken driving when suddenly he puts the brakes on and comes to a complete stop. About 30 yards away from us was a twelve-foot (at least) alligator lying in the sun with his jaws wide open and his eyes closed. His skin was gray and completely dried out. He looked like something you might see displayed at an amusement park or resort, magnificent and ugly. We got out of the cart and gawked at it. Our friends had also stopped, and the four of us just stood there looking at it. After a moment, Ken said, "I don't think it's real." No one else said anything. We couldn't stop staring at it. Ken takes a golf ball and throws it at the alligator, hitting him in the shoulder area. The ball flopped down right by the alligator's head. The alligator never moved. Never opened his eyes, not even a twitch. "I don't think he's real," said Ken once again. And I said, "Then go get the ball." The ball is right by the reptile's head. If he really believed that the alligator was not real, then what was the problem?

Ken ignored me. He grabbed a club from his golf bag. Why? Because he's not too bright. He circled behind the alligator, giving as wide a berth as he could and hit the alligator on the back of its long tail. Whack! Then he ran as fast as he could back around to the rest of us. The alligator didn't move. Nothing.

"I don't think it's real!" Ken repeated. And I couldn't help myself, replying, "Then go get the ball!" If you really believe it, then take action.

Finally, our friend Dan took a ball out of his pocket, grabbed his putter and hit the ball as hard as he could. The ball hit the alligator on the side of his face. Immediately the alligator sprung into action as he twisted and turned quicker than we would have ever thought. He looked down and swallowed the golf ball that had been laying by his head. The four of us squealed like little kids, jumped in our carts, and raced away as fast as we could. I guess it was real.

The Foundation Principle requires us to believe so strongly in our values that we are willing to take action, to go get the ball. So often we say we believe things but take no intentional action, no risk to live into what we say to be true. Driving through fog inherently requires risk.

I encourage you to do a behavior audit along with your narrative and value audit. Many of our behaviors are habits because just like our brain likes to create stories, it also likes to automate actions. Habits are ingrained and routines may be hard to notice in ourselves. Again this is where the insight of a trusted community is indispensable. Along with habits, think about some actions you've taken over the past month. What actions are you proud of? What actions do you regret? Taking time to reflect on what motivation drove your actions is priceless. When we get to the root, it's easier to pull up the whole plant of our actions and make the changes necessary.

Create a list of your core behaviors. Which ones are positive for you and which ones are negative? Look at them in light of your values and narratives. What matches and what doesn't? What do you want to change? Then create a list of behaviors you want to replace them with. Brain science tells us it's much easier to replace a habit than quit a habit. As we align our habits with our values and narratives, we hope to start new habits and actions that will drive us forward on the right path through the fog.

Conclusion

I know this is hard work, but we are building a foundation. If we don't get the foundation right, the entire house can fall. Getting the foundation of my values, narratives, and behaviors set in place changed my life. And of course they aren't permanently set but can change over time. The point is to know our values, understand our narratives, and align our behaviors. When these find synergy, we are able to move forward with a stronger momentum than we may have thought possible.

It is possible to find direction in the fog. It is

possible to move forward when the wind is knocked out of you and you feel like you can't get back up. In the midst of disorientation we can reorient and build a foundation so we can keep driving and keep our lives moving forward to our desired destination.

IMPLEMENTATION QUESTIONS

In the Foundation Principle we have seen that the alignment of our values, narrative, and behavior ground us to be able to drive through any fog. One of the keys to solidifying this footing is to intentionally define all three components.

1. What is most valuable to you? Write down things that are important to you and narrow them down to the five or six things that you value the most. Some examples are: investing in others, always learning, generosity, etc.
2. What has been the narrative in your life? Some examples are: critical of others, hopeful encouragement, negative about life, inconsistent dependent on situations, etc. What do you want your narrative to be and what kind of narrative aligns with your values?
3. What habits and actions are misaligned and aligned with your values? Write

down actions you might take to be more aligned.
4. To build momentum requires a focused intensity over time. What are you focused on with intensity? Do your values, narrative, and behavior match up with that particular focus?

Chapter 2
The Priority Principle

RECOMMENDED LISTENING AS YOU DRIVE:
Wishing Fountains by Bad Suns
Missing Piece by Vance Joy

Bringing Focus in the Fog

The flight to Asheville was delayed about four hours. Heavy fog with snow has a way of doing that. As I got my rental car, I double-checked my directions. Apparently I needed to drive 90 minutes up the mountain to a sleepy little town with a small no-name hotel that would house me for the night. It was a bit past midnight and visibility was at a minimum. As I drove up the winding road, it took me half an hour to realize that my GPS had no clue where I was going. It would tell me to turn right on roads that were non-existent and to turn left on roads that are only open in the summer. I was completely lost. Not only lost, but my consulting client did not leave a phone number to call. The realization rested heavily: "No one can help me and no one knows where I am. I am all alone."

When you are driving through fog, two things have the potential to derail you.

One is that you isolate yourself from others. Sometimes the pain and stress or the lack of knowing what is ahead can paralyze us socially. We may pull away from others. We become self-oriented, almost obsessed with the fog. We can't see others metaphorically and literally.

Two is that driving through fog can make us resentful toward others. Just like moisture produces mold, a lack of clarity tends to produce resentment. We think that no one cares and that people are jerks. Maybe we blame others, or perhaps we are embarrassed or filled with shame at the fog we find ourselves in. In our shame and fear we turn our resentment outwards rather than living with the inward pain. Or maybe we succumb to both.

It can be hard to believe that people are the greatest resource we have to move forward. They feel like obstacles in the way rather than an opportunity for a way out.

What do you believe about people?

When my son was little, maybe 4 or 5 years old, he was outside playing when all of a sudden we could hear music coming down the street. It was loud and repetitive, kind of fun and carnival sounding. You know what I am talking about? It was the ice cream truck! And if you think about it, ice cream trucks are super creepy. The ice cream man driving as slowly as possible, looking to make eye contact with small children, luring them to run and get some money so that they can put mass quantities of sugar in them, usually at about 10 a.m.

But in this case, I noticed that my son, Connor, didn't know what an ice cream truck was or who the ice cream man was. The perfect target. All he knew was a music truck was heading our way. He just sat there with his eyes wide and his mouth open. If he fully understood what it was, he would have already been in pure unashamed begging mode. But he sat there in awe of the music.

As the truck got closer I was at a loss as to what to do. His mother came to the rescue. She said, "Connor, do you like the music truck?" He nodded his head as he looked on in wonder.

Sure, I thought, after all it is a truck and it plays music. Situation averted.

A few days after this incident, Connor came rushing into the house at top speed. He was holding one of those Rocket Pops about the size of his head. He was shaking like a leaf. I don't know if it was excitement or the sugar hitting his bloodstream.

"Mommy, Mommy," he said. "There is ice cream in the music truck!"

Turns out that one of our neighbors decided to educate him on the realities of music trucks. Connor just wanted to make sure that his mother knew that there was more to it than she thought. There's more, and it's great!

That's how it is with people. There is more than we might think. More potential. More skill. There is always MORE. Often people just need someone to believe in them and to invest in them. Whatever assumptions we make are grossly inadequate to the goodness inside.

Will you stop and ask the question: What do I really believe about people?

In the fog, the tendency is to have all of our thoughts and actions be about ourselves. Where do I go? What do I do? How am I feeling?

What if the way out of the fog is to prioritize people?

I believe people are brilliant and that often when someone believes in them, they shine. Like stars, they are always shining, we just have to unobscure our vision and notice. Could it be that the way forward out of the fog is more about getting our eyes off of ourselves and investing in people, bringing the brilliance out of them, than it is about displaying our own brilliance or finding the exact right solution?

When we don't know the path forward, the priority is always other people.

We can prioritize people in two ways. The first is initiating with them, and the second is by serving them.

The Power of Initiating

One February I was in North Carolina. My work takes me to different parts of the country, and I was in the western part of the state for a couple of days. On the last day, it began to snow. In Illinois, where I am from, we don't skip a beat. Snow? What's the big deal? It's a part of life. In North Carolina I learned snow is always a red-alert full meltdown! And this was apocalyptic snow: three to five inches. You would have thought the world was coming to an end. There was no bread or milk at any grocery store, which has never made sense to me. Why milk and bread? Why not water and meat?

I had planned to connect with about ten people from all around the region. Some from sixty miles away. Our plans were immediately canceled. No way any of them were going to come. For some reason, three to five inches of snow is drivable in Chicago but undrivable in North Carolina. At about noon, I decided to go ahead and get to the airport and see when I could get a flight back home. I was about an hour away from Charlotte, and as I got on the road I noticed a couple of things.

One was that very few people were on the road. Practically no one. They were all at home eating bread and drinking milk. As I drove I got on a four-lane highway and right away found myself behind a snowplow. Great! It was going about forty-five miles per hour, which I thought was fine. Snow was blowing everywhere and still falling, but I was behind a snowplow. I did this for about 20 miles. It was easy, I just took my time and everything was good.

Until suddenly, the snowplow took an exit ramp. Immediately everything changed. There was a fresh four inches of snow on the ground, and no one had gone before me. There were no tracks and no cars in front of me. My first reaction was to slow down a little but fear crept up as I didn't know what was underneath the snow. As the wind became stronger I became more focused and more concerned. I wished I was next to a warm fireplace eating bread and drinking milk. When no one is in front of you and you have to go first, it can be scary. Being out on your own and leading the way inevitably makes you uncomfortable.

When we talk about prioritizing people we are talking about making the path and initiating with others. Reaching out to others. Plowing forward even though we long to follow someone else's path.

It is the only way we fight the tendencies of isolation and resentment. We don't know what will happen, but we must go first. It is different from following someone or something that goes before us. It is the path of priority for us, the path forward, the path that eventually leads us to a life of hope.

For me, the deepest fog of my life was also the loneliest time of my life. It felt as if all the stability had been taken away from me and I was all by myself. Have you ever felt like that? Like all the friendships and relationships in your life just vanish?

It was during this season that I learned a valuable lesson. If you initiate with others, you move forward. The use of energy away from myself moved me further into the fog, which would eventually lead me out. If you initiate, you win.

But what do we do when we initiate? Do we scream for help? Do we ask them to drive us through the fog?

The late bestselling author and leadership expert Jason Jennings would challenge people with an exercise that can give us some insight into moving forward.

Get alone with no one else around. Then put yourself in front of a mirror. I don't know if you've ever noticed but it's really hard to lie to yourself when you are looking at yourself. It's hard to justify or be defensive when your eyes are looking back at you. As you look at yourself, ask this question:

Is my life going to be about me, or is my life going to be about others?

Then ask it again:

Is my life going to be about me, or is my life going to be about others?

The question may be easy to ask but not easy to answer. As I look forward and don't know what tomorrow holds, is my life going to be defined by scarcity or abundance?

The truthful answer changes everything.

When Jesus walked the earth, so many of his fellow people were governed by a litany of rules and regulations. The path forward was filled by a lack of visibility with different priorities surfacing through countless causes and needs. There was oppression and discord. Division and violent expression. So much fear and uncertainty. Does all of that sound familiar? It sounds like our time today. In the midst of the fog, the voice of Jesus can be heard.

Jesus said, A new command I give you: Love one another. As I have loved you, so you must love one another. (John 13:34)

That simply and succinctly defines living life for others. And it gives us our priority.

Relationships Drive

Life's experiences can put us into an isolated and resentful state, where we want to settle down into the fog, never moving forward. That's certainly where I was as I sat on the living room floor. I had a promise that God would "lead the blind, by ways they have not known," but what was my life going to be about? Was it going to be about me? Or others? Like fuel in a car, relationships drive us forward.

One of the great opportunities of driving in the fog is the purposeful decision about what we will prioritize. It became clear to me in the midst of the uncertainty and the fear of the unknown that serving others was the only way to prioritize people. I don't know how long it took me to get up off the living room floor, but I decided that no matter what else was going on, I was going to intentionally serve someone every day. Initiate with the intent of serving. It's easier to initiate for selfish reasons or personal benefit. But a heart to serve is the heartbeat of prioritizing people.

Choosing to serve others will inevitably help us drive through the fog. What does serving others look like? I challenge you to think big and think small. Sometimes we need to dive straight into the deep end and start with big opportunities to serve. Other times we may need to employ the small step, one foot in front of the other mentality.

What are small ways within your power to serve people? Buying someone a coffee? Holding open a door? Making time to visit the friend you haven't seen in a while or you know is going through a hard time? Maybe it's making yourself available to volunteer at your church or a local nonprofit you believe in.

Maybe you've been neglecting an area in your life where you know you need to serve. Spending quality time with a family member. Consistently helping the coworker who struggles with an aspect of the job or organization. Taking the leap to help a stranger even though it may be awkward at first. Or maybe the biggest leap of all is serving those we like the least. Jesus counseled his followers to love their enemies, and I believe it's good counseling for us.

No matter how big or small, if we can consistently keep our eyes looking for ways to serve others, our personal happiness scale increases. It goes back to the paradoxical teaching of Jesus that it is truly better to give than it is to receive. It's less about coming up with a type A five-point plan to serve others than it is about having a posture of service whenever the opportunity arises. When we make our priority to serve others in our relational context, then serving others will drive our priority.

It's also not about getting it perfect or never missing an opportunity. If we make perfection our expectation we will never start in the first place. We are all imperfect, all have selfish moments, and all miss chances to help others. We aren't personal nonprofit organizations, and we aren't servant robots. But we are humans, and we are made to care for and love one another. The power of community can hardly be overstated.

Ultimately it's all about shifting our focus. When our focus shifts from us to others, we gain a surprising level of clarity, confidence, and momentum.

Conclusion

The point is this: In whatever fog we find ourselves in, the priority is people. Relationships are the most important thing. And when we prioritize people by initiating with them and serving them, we see the brilliance of others; we see that there is more to them. There is always more. Relationships rescue us from our self-focus and resentment.

Here is the challenge to applying the Priority Principle. The challenge is to create an investment plan. Not a financial investment plan, although this plan also creates long-term dividends. The investment plan I am talking about is an intentional approach to investing in others. Whatever fog you are in, I challenge you to intentionally invest in others.

Make a list of people who are in your life (or who you want to invest more in). Write down how often you want to initiate and serve them.

Think through what it might look like to invest in them. What amount of time and energy does it require? If you are a person of faith, begin to pray for them daily. Put these investments into your calendar and begin to do it. Sometimes we have to force our body to take the actions we want our minds to take in order for our minds to catch up.

What we find when we live by the Priority Principle may surprise us. History, as captured in John 20, tells us of a woman named Mary who was a disciple of Jesus. She had witnessed the death of her teacher and Lord and stood crying outside of the tomb that he had been buried in. The tomb was empty, and as she looked in, she saw that there was no body. Is nothing sacred, why would someone steal his body? As she sobbed, she saw a man that she assumed was the gardener. She didn't recognize him. "Sir, if you have carried him away, tell me where you have put him and I will get him," she said. The man called her by name, "Mary." It was then that she recognized him. It was Jesus, raised from the dead. In that recognition, nothing else mattered. You see, with Jesus, there was more. There's always more.

IMPLEMENTATION QUESTIONS

In the Priority Principle we overcome the temptation to either isolate or resent people. Instead, we move forward by initiating and serving others.

1. Ask yourself the challenging question: Is my life going to be about me or is my life going to be about others? What needs to change if my priority is going to be others?
2. How good are you at initiating with others? What could you consistently do to get better at going first?
3. Where and how is serving others a part of your daily life?
4. Who do you want to invest yourself into? Make a list and begin intentionally investing.

Chapter 3
The Wisdom Principle

RECOMMENDED LISTENING AS YOU DRIVE:
City of Blinding Lights by U2
The Walk Home by Young the Giant

Making Decisions in the Fog

When you are driving through fog, there is one commodity that can easily be missing: wisdom. A quick internet search tells me that wisdom is the soundness of an action or decision with regard to the application of experience, knowledge, and good judgment. Wisdom involves the cognitive ability to think in current situations coupled with the self-awareness to know how that situation affects us, resulting in a decision with a positive outcome. In other words, wisdom deals with the ability to make a decision with the knowledge and awareness of current circumstances.

Under normal circumstances wisdom is really hard to find. No wonder there are so many proverbs and ancient writings about the value of pursuing and gaining wisdom. Proverbs 4:6 tells us, "The beginning of wisdom is this: Get wisdom. Though it costs all you have, get understanding."

And that's just normal circumstances. When you are driving through fog, wisdom becomes essential and yet elusive. We have data but the circumstances shift in how we might use that information. Making a decision with the right data is easier said than done.

Our phones have become a primary source of information. Studies show the average person uses their smartphone 3 hours and 15 minutes a day. Over two-thirds of that time is spent on the internet. You and I probably know people who spend a lot more time than that on their phone. Or maybe, if we are being honest, it's us. One of the great resources of our phones are the GPS apps. I actually have three different apps that will help me get directions from where I am to where I want to go. Why three? You never know when you might need another one.

One winter day I was driving through the Blue Ridge Mountains in North Carolina. It's a beautiful part of the world, and I was on my way to speak at a retreat center where I would see and experience mountainous beauty for the entire weekend. My rental car had Apple CarPlay connected, and my phone screen was transported to a much larger screen for easy access. It was getting dark outside, and I was climbing up a two-lane road with little visibility when suddenly I lost internet service. The GPS directions stopped.

After a few minutes, there was a little shoulder for me to pull into. I double and triple checked each of my three GPS apps. Nothing. No connection and no guidance on my final destination. I knew the direction that I needed to go, but my circumstances had changed. I knew the direction, but I no longer *had* the directions. I was going up the mountain but to what destination? Where do I turn? What is up ahead? My circumstances changed the way that I was going to drive.

Similarly, circumstances challenge our use of knowledge as we drive through our personal fog. Clear directions are often replaced by stress. Our brains are wired to be more reactionary under stress. So naturally in foggy situations, we quickly react and often make bad decisions. Our normal levels of wisdom are affected by the stress that our personal fog causes. It's like a GPS that loses connection. It's hard to tell where you are and where you want to go.

It's hard to find something that's more important or that changes our trajectory in life more than the decisions we make. Whether it's where we live, what we do, who we do it with—all these major decisions. And then there's a million little decisions within that.

What is the impact stress has on you? Have you ever tracked the influence that trauma or even anxiety can have on you and the decisions you make?

When we are faced with unexpected fog, we have certain physical and emotional responses. They are influenced by our personality, history, and habits.

Think about the GPS and how it relates to our physical and emotional responses.

As I sat on the shoulder of the road, I found myself suddenly angry. I was yelling. I'm not sure who I was yelling at, but I got loud. I felt helpless and out of control. My mind began to think in extremes. "I'm never going to get there. This always happens to me." It was not pretty, and it's humbling and surprising how quickly I can switch from inner calm to outward rage.

My heart rate climbed, and my immediate reaction was to make an impulsive decision. "Should I just go back? I know the general direction; I'll just drive without specific directions. I can make it, even though I've never been here before and it's dark in the mountains." I had no idea how to make a decision. On the wisdom side of driving through the fog, decision-making is huge.

I believe that's what happens when you're driving through the fog in life. You think, "I used to know how to make decisions. Right now, the simplest decisions don't make sense to me because I can't see where I'm going. I can't see where the curve is, I can't see where the end of the road is, I can't see where other cars are, and I can't see in any of the directions I used to."

The point is this: When driving through fog, decision-making is difficult because wisdom is hard to find. The principle of wisdom, finding and choosing understanding, is key to driving through fog.

There are two types of wise decisions that need to be made when circumstances change. The first is intentionally choosing how we will wisely deal with adversity. The second is deciding how we will overcome the biggest obstacles to moving forward.

Wisdom in Adversity

We can lead ourselves and others by learning how to make decisions in the face of adversity.

There are two essential decisions that need to be made in order to move forward through adversity. The first of those has to do with character.

When interviewed before a big fight, Mike Tyson famously said, "Everyone has a plan until they get punched in the mouth." Have you ever been punched in the mouth?

I don't mean literally (although that might be

true as well). We have plans, strategies, expectations—and then the punch comes. It might come in the form of a broken relationship, a lost job, or a health issue. It can come by pursuing something and then realizing it's not what you thought it was. It's about failing when we expect success.

This book started on the living room floor with me having lost both a career and a marriage. All my plans and dreams were dissipating before my eyes. I got punched in the mouth. And the gut. And the groin. When you are on the receiving end of a punch, and all of us are at one point or another, you learn a lot about who you are. You learn a lot about your true character.

I used to believe that adversity *develops* character. And that is true to some extent. But more than anything else, adversity *reveals* character. What is in you when you get punched in the mouth, so to speak? Hardship is an X-ray for our character.

How will you deal with adversity?

Thomas Bandy, in his book "Spiritual Leadership", speaks of four on-going threats to life. Four threats that emerge in adversity and bring anxiety. These threats are constant enemies to hope. In the midst of any fog, they are present, and truth be known, they never really leave us. We don't always experience them, but they are lurking behind any and all adversity. These threats are depression, dread, anger, and abandonment.[1]

Depression and its brother discouragement result from being lost and forgotten. When I was on the living room floor, the loneliness tempted me to wallow in self-pity and self-centeredness. I truly felt lost, forgotten, and relationally isolated.

Dread comes to me when I try to predict what is on the other side of the fog before I can actually see anything. It becomes a "worst case scenario thinking" and a doom-and-gloom mentality. Left to itself, dread results in dogmatism, legalism, and arrogance as if we know what is coming and everyone who thinks differently is wrong. I find that adversity can paralyze me with fear when dread goes unchecked.

Anger is present when we feel powerless and wronged. Does adversity make us lash out towards ourselves, others, or God?

Abandonment is more prevalent in our lives than we may be aware of. It is easy in the fog to feel forgotten, even betrayed. Rejection runs deep in all of us as none has been loved perfectly.

When moving forward through the fog, it is critical that we stop and engage with how adversity is affecting us. Does depression threaten to take over? Is dread consuming my thinking? Am I lashing out in anger and overreacting to people and situations? Are the feelings of abandonment threatening my well-being?

Adversity reveals character and it beckons us to choose how we will deal with these on-going threats. Our choice is a sign of our character.

With that in mind, here is a character test in the midst of driving through fog:

- Is depression paralyzing me and keeping me from living an aligned life where I prioritize people?
- Am I looking toward the future with anxiety and dread?
- Does anger dominate my interactions with others or my imagined interactions with others? Do I have sudden, uncontrolled outbursts of anger?
- Have I believed that no one is there for me and that I have been abandoned?

When the stress of adversity begins to impact us, it is important that we make wise choices. These decisions bring us to a place where character is both revealed and formed. Wisdom in the face of stress looks as follows:

Step 1: Choose to Engage

There are many choices that we can make to escape the impact of adversity. Some obvious escapes include alcohol abuse, sexual encounters, maybe even extravagant purchases or trips. But over the years, I have also seen many people choose to escape their pain by blaming others and moving on too quickly by diving into new adventures without ever engaging with the fog.

My friend Mark came home to a mostly empty house and a note. Apparently, his wife was unhappy and left abruptly. Suddenly he was in the deepest fog he had ever known and never asked for. He quickly fell into depression, dread, anger, and abandonment all at the same time. A few friends told him to get a lawyer, grab all the money, etc. In many ways, they say, "the solution is to enrage rather than engage!" Mark is not normally an angry, vindictive person. But at that moment, he faced a choice point.

He couldn't choose or control whether or not he experienced these threats, but he could choose, over time, to either act on them or to connect with the overwhelming combination of information and emotion. Much has been written on the power of grief, and I will not dive into it here, but I will say that character is never developed by escaping pain. It is essential, rather, to stop and feel. To be true to the values, narrative, and behaviors we talked about in the Foundation Principle. Leaning into pain is wise even though it may not be the natural direction our GPS takes us.

For me, it was time on the living room floor with a journal processing the unsolvable emotions.

Praying when possible, talking to others when appropriate, and engaging with adversity allows for character to deepen and continue to develop.

Step 2: Choose to Trust

It is not enough to engage with the threats of our fog. Another choice is in front of us as we deal with adversity. Will we choose to trust or not? To have great character requires having wisdom in who and how we trust.

"What is one piece of advice you would give me?" A great question asked by a twenty-two-year-old graduate student sitting in a room with ten women and men all in their forties and fifties. Much of the advice given was not as helpful as hoped. However, one of the older women in the group gave a nugget of wisdom that stopped everyone in their tracks. "Trust people," she said. "They will let you down. Trust them anyway." After what seemed like a couple of minutes of complete silence, she explained her advice. "Life will tempt you to never trust anyone, but you can't love if you don't figure out a way to trust."

I'm still wrestling with the wisdom of these profound words. For me as a person of faith, it starts with trusting God. As we drive through the fog, we long for peace and joy to be a part of the journey. In the midst of adversity, they seem to be elusive.

Romans 15:13 tells us the one choice of wisdom that makes all the difference. It says, "May the God of hope fill you with all joy and peace as you *trust* him...."

Joy and peace come from one choice. One decision lived out in adversity. Trust.

This also applies to people. Trust is not ignorant or naive. Trust is wise. Trusting people does not mean we believe they are perfect or they will not hurt us. Trusting people is a choice to love people and to allow people to love us. A closed heart is one of the greatest and most dangerous temptations of the fog. A closed heart creates more fog and an open heart of trust pierces the fog.

Trust is not a natural inclination for happy people but a choice for wise people. Choose to trust and connect with people.

Step 3: Choose to Embrace the Paradox

Before I faced major adversity, I believed that life was either going well or going poorly. It was good weather or bad weather. In good weather, you go forward, and in bad weather, you wait for the storm to pass. But in adversity, there is fog and we still need to move forward. Good and bad dichotomies are not helpful in the complexity of the fog. We need to be able to accept the paradoxical existence of both the good and the bad.

The character lesson I learned in the fog is that the four threats of depression, dread, anger, and abandonment are present, but they shrink as I engage with the pain and trust God. Both pain and tremendous joy are present as we drive through the fog. It's a paradox. Wisdom comes from embracing the authenticity of both.

Delegitimizing pain is the source of many of our struggles with mental and emotional health. Relationships and situations are never completely good or one hundred percent evil even when they feel like it. If we villainize or deify people, we are the ones who inevitably will be hurt.

Nuanced approaches to viewing people and situations are not easy. Picking a side and sticking to it without conversation and contemplation is one of the reasons why we have so much division today. If you want to decrease conflict in your life, both internally and externally, choose to embrace the paradox.

Step 4: Choose to Impact Others

One of the challenges that I see in driving through fog is that we don't have contact with others who can show us how to do it. There are great stories of victory and we see the failures around us, but are there relatable role models?

On May 16, 2008, Anthony Rizzo, a top prospect for the Boston Red Sox, met Jon Lester, a starting pitcher on the same team. The introduction was life-changing for Rizzo in that he had just been diagnosed with cancer, something that Lester was more than familiar with. Jon had just come out of successful chemotherapy and had recently been declared cancer free.

As Lester answered Anthony's questions, he simply told his story, reassured Rizzo that he would not be alone, and explained what Rizzo should expect as he drove through his own personal fog.[2]

Little did either of them know that they would start a relationship that would culminate in 2016 as they played significant roles in bringing a championship to my beloved Chicago Cubs.

Jon Lester never took away the pain and adversity of Anthony Rizzo's cancer. But he provided what all of us need as we drive through the fog: a role model. Someone who has been there and has made it to the other side. In my fog, I struggled to find a role model, but that doesn't mean that now I can't choose to be that for someone else. It's a choice to be there for others. And you can be intentional and choose to find your role model. It may take a while but keep pursuing a role model. It may impact the trajectory of your life or career in unimaginable ways. Choose to impact others by finding a role model and being a role model.

Taking Action

The second wise decision in dealing with adversity is the choice to take action.

The stress of not being able to see what is up ahead can make us want to pull over on the side of the road and be paralyzed with inaction. The most action-oriented people can suddenly struggle to find any energy and be afraid to take any action. Rightly so, they don't want to act impulsive or foolishly. And yet there are certain types of actions that are critical while driving through fog.

For homeowners, one of the worst sounds is dripping water. This is exactly what I heard as I went into the storage room in our basement one day. Along with boxes and seasonal decorations, the storage room is where our furnace, water heater, and other utilities are located. Along the back wall of the room run water lines that connect from the rest of the house. One of those water lines is a thin hose coming from the refrigerator in our kitchen. It was leaking. Only a bit but it was steady. Drip, drip, drip. I swear, all I did was touch it. One finger on the connector and bam! Water shot out from the line like a firehose straight into my face. And of course right into my eyes!

What do you do? I screamed! Loudly! A constant scream. My wife, Judy, came running down the stairs while I covered my face and tried to cover the hole where water was shooting out. Judy frantically grabbed towels and ran to grab our neighbor who is good at household repairs. With the neighbor's help, we were able to find the water shut-off valve and turn the water off. The whole experience lasted less than ten minutes. As I told the story of the unexpected water blasting me in the face, both my wife and neighbor could not stop laughing. I'm glad I could amuse them.

There are some occurrences in life that require a certain sense of urgency. Action must be taken immediately. There is no waiting. There is no debating. There is only action without delay.

The late Jason Jennings was one of the world's leading experts in growth, speed, and change. One of his books is titled "It's Not the Big that Eat the Small but the Fast that Eat the Slow."

One lesson from that book is important here: If you know what to do, why would you do it slowly?

Driving through fog can make us second-guess things that we know are right. Potentially we stop taking action in specific areas that require immediate movement. If you're in crisis, more than likely immediate movement is required.

Some questions I have learned to ask in fog include:

- Am I hesitating to do what I know is right?
- Am I moving slowly when I need to move quickly?
- If I was advising someone on this crisis, what would I tell them to do?

Here are some action steps that are important to take.

Physical Upkeep

A therapist once urged me to work out in the middle of a particularly foggy season. He insisted that I work out to the point of holding me accountable and pushing me to not only take care of myself physically but to punish stress by giving it an outlet. When we are stressed and fogged out, we need to take the immediate action of getting our bodies moving. It's amazing how our minds can clear when we get our bodies moving. This physical exercise is not a one-size-fits-all solution. Start where you are and start with what you enjoy.

Do you enjoy team sports and being social? Try a group for basketball, softball, or pickleball. Would you rather take time in solitude with running or walking? That's great too. When we do something consistently over time that brings us joy, it will have a much greater impact on our lives.

Physical upkeep also includes our food and sleep. Taking care of our bodies in stressful times is the last thing that many people are motivated to do, but it is crucial. What we put into our bodies is our fuel and can dramatically affect our food and physical energy. What are you eating? Would it be helpful to work with a nutritionist or talk with a friend to help you revamp your diet? Small changes can make a big difference. For some of us, it may be eating new things, and for others it may be to stop eating a particular food.

Finally, ask yourself, how are you sleeping? Do you think this affects your fog? What can you immediately do to improve or increase your sleep? A well-rested body and mind can make a world of difference.

Moral Intentionality

Who do you aspire to be on the other side of the fog? Choosing to be someone who doesn't blame others or is negative and rage-filled is a choice in the midst of the fog. This is a choice I had to make or I believe I would have naturally drifted there.

Perhaps you know people who have gone through a horrible season and became angry and bitter. Or after that horrible season, they found themselves isolated from everyone by the choices they made. Over time you see that their adversity changed them. The things we do, do something to us—they shape the people we become. Choosing to complain, criticize, play the victim, and focus on the negative will shape the people we become. That is why it is crucial to make choices and create habits while we are driving through the fog that form the change we long to have.

What immediate action do you need to take to chart your course toward becoming the moral and intentional person you want to be?

Relational Inclusion

In the fog, there is an urgency of action on who we will include with us and who we will exclude. Let me take us back to the living room floor where I sat and did a mental autopsy on my career and marriage. One thing I am grateful for is the advice I was given to choose with whom I surrounded myself. Some people were not very good connections for me to have. They brought me back to pain, back to anger. Certain people I actually needed to avoid. Other friends were life giving. I had one friend in particular I chose to include. For a period of six weeks, he called me every day. He would ask, "How was today? What did you do? How did it go?" Some days I didn't have the energy to talk to him. I'd just let his call go to voicemail. One day he left the following voicemail: "I got one word for you today: windshield. Windshield. No more rear view mirror. Windshield."

It was powerful. Driving through the fog does require more energy moving forward than looking at what's behind you. Purposefully including others as we drive is a choice of wisdom, and you never know what wisdom they may give as a result.

Perhaps you have heard of Sam Bennett, a talented amateur golfer from Madisonville, Texas, who took on the best players in the world at his first Masters. His journey is incredibly inspiring.

When Sam was in high school, his father, Mark, was diagnosed with early onset Alzheimer's disease. Despite the challenges, Sam decided to follow in his father's footsteps and enrolled at Texas A&M, his father's alma mater, to pursue his passion for golf.

As Mark's health declined, he imparted some wise words to Sam that would stay with him forever: "Don't wait to do something."

Sam took these words to heart and got them tattooed on his forearm as a reminder. Sadly, Mark passed away in June 2021. However, a year later, Sam achieved a remarkable feat by winning the U.S. Amateur Championship, which earned him a spot in the prestigious Masters Tournament. He was even paired with the defending champion and world's top golfer, Scottie Scheffler.

Photo courtesy of Sam Bennett

Sam's performance at the Masters was exceptional, and he was awarded the esteemed "Low Amateur" honor, a remarkable achievement for his first appearance in the tournament. As part of his pre-shot routine, Sam looks at this tattoo, a reminder of the love and wisdom of his father.[3]

When driving through fog, decision making is difficult because wisdom is hard to find. The principle of wisdom, finding and choosing understanding, is key to driving through fog. There are two types of wise decisions that need to be made. The first is intentionally deciding how we will deal with adversity. These are choices of character and choices of action.

Wisdom in Overcoming Obstacles

Secondly, wisdom is needed in deciding how we will overcome the biggest obstacles to moving forward.

I'm convinced the biggest obstacles to momentum are complexity, control, complacency, and concern. If we get tangled up in any one of these, our momentum in moving forward can immediately come to a halt. But there are solutions to each which allow us to regain our momentum.

Complexity to Simplicity

Life is complex. It just is. And complexity in our lives is easy. Just keep adding things and it is bound to get complex.

Nicole is a spiritual entrepreneur who started a church in the southeast part of the United States. It started with a handful of people committed to the spiritual and physical well-being of the community. They opened their doors and over the course of the next three years grew to about two hundred people who served the needs of their town, caring for the under-resourced and gathering together on Sundays. It was simple and it was energizing. But then Nicole and her leaders decided to add programs for their students, for new people, and other groups of people. Those were all good and natural steps to growth. But they had unwanted consequences. Seemingly overnight the organization became overly complex. Communication became difficult, relationships became strained, and finances were depleted. Complex became complicated. And complicated is fog-inducing.

So it is on an individual level as well. Nicole found herself struggling to find simple. She found what Steve Jobs once said to be true. He said, "Simple can be harder than complex: You have to work hard to get your thinking clean to make it simple. But it's worth it in the end because once you get there, you can move mountains."[4]

In the midst of this fog Nicole worked hard to move forward with this in mind: Things may be complex, but I need to find simple action steps.

How do you make a simple action plan when a situation is complex? We usually give complex answers to complex situations, but we actually need a simple answer to a complex situation. The key is this: Focusing on the first move and then the second move will help you figure out what you need to do for the next step after that. Let go of the temptation to think fifteen steps ahead; start with three to five.

For complexity, the solution to keep moving forward is to aim for simplicity—getting to small, simple action steps. When we break down a situation into simple and manageable action, we are able to keep moving forward.

If you're in a fog and feel overwhelmed, don't

worry about solving all of your problems. That will feel overwhelming. Just do the next right thing and go from there.

Controlling to Releasing

Along with complexity, there is control. I think everyone has control issues of some kind. They surface in different ways. Some are very obvious; others are sneaky. We like to feel in control of things, especially when we can't see where we are going. But control is an illusion that gives us a false sense of power and peace.

When you're driving through the fog, you have no control. You're not sure where you're going, so you can't really control it. The more we try to control things, the more anxious and overwhelmed we become. That's the funny thing about control—the more we try to get it, the more things and situations slip away from us.

The remedy to controlling is releasing. This involves both letting go and letting others. The only way to be able to release things is to address the spiritual issue that's underneath it. We often want control because we want power, but we must learn to let go of power through surrender. Surrender is a spiritual issue. Am I going to be in control or will I allow God to be in control? Personally, I'm not sure someone can let go without the help and reassurance of God's power and control.

Releasing also involves engaging others and letting them have control either partially or wholly. You ask other people to take whatever it is you're holding onto. Sometimes that is practical, such as tasks or responsibilities that others can help with. Other times it is emotional or spiritual, such as asking someone to pray for you or listen to your struggles. As I write this, a friend of mine comes to mind. He is sick. Potentially very sick. As he navigates through his fog, he struggles to let go. He quietly tries to control it—when releasing may look like letting others carry the burden with him.

This practice of giving away power is so helpful in our acceptance of the fog and the limitations we all have as humans. The obstacle of control is deadly in the fog and causes many people to become stuck in their own obsessions and rejection of reality. The power of letting go and letting others when driving through the fog cannot be overstated.

Complacency to Passion

Complacency is the third obstacle. And it can be daunting. After a while, you get so tired in the fog. It feels like it will never end and you've come to the end of your own wit and willpower. Especially when you don't care anymore and apathy becomes your new normal. Apathy just wears you out to the point you don't have energy to think or take action. Apathy can feel like our personal damp and heavy cloud that shrouds our entire existence.

I learned a long time ago not to ask people who are in the fog what they are passionate about. Because they don't know how to answer. People in all stages and situations have a hard time defining their passions anyway, but they don't know how to answer it when they're in the fog. It's like asking a person what's on the other side of a ten-foot concrete wall they've never looked over. Sometimes people even get mad at the question. It may seem like they're mad at you, but they are actually mad at themselves because we all desire to be passionate and desire to live life to the full. But passion can be elusive. Some of us feel like we are passionate about nothing, and others feel like they are passionate about everything. Both can lead to apathy.

Instead I think we need to focus on how we build commitment. Because passion is an output not an input. You can't decide to be a passionate person. Passion is the result of a deep commitment to someone or something. That's how we get passionate. Passion is an output of commitment. So the counterpart to complacency is doing a lot of work to make commitments and decide what you want to be committed to. Ask yourself, "What am I committed to in this season?" Again, people can commit to a few things or too many things but both have the same end result.

Allow passion and energy to flow from your commitment. The concerning part is the fear that paralyzes people. There's a need to overcome the idol of clarity, meaning clarity becomes necessary to take any steps. At least that's what it's been for me. I won't move unless I can see with complete clarity, and I think that's an idol that impedes rather than a reality that helps.

Many people came to Mother Teresa asking for prayer and advice about awful and confusing life situations. Mother Teresa said she doesn't pray for clarity for anyone because clarity is a crutch to the Christian. And I would add to someone living in the fog. But Mother Teresa would pray that the person's trust in God would increase. Clarity may never be possible but trust is always possible.[5]

Another helpful way to think about it is the concept of twenty seconds of courage. In the movie *We Bought a Zoo*, the main character, Benjamin (played by Matt Damon), is talking to his teenage son, Dylan. In encouraging his son to do a hard thing, he tells him he doesn't have to be brave—he just needs twenty seconds of courage.

Sometimes twenty seconds is all it takes. That hard thing Dylan is talking to his dad about is asking a girl out. And it's the first time he's confiding in his dad that he likes this girl.[6] I think Benjamin's wisdom is genius. Sometimes in life, all it takes is twenty seconds of courage. I think that's a big, big deal. And that's wisdom to me, knowing when you actually need to step in and say, "Okay, I know what to do; I just have to go for it. I don't need to have all the answers or a plan, but I do need to do this thing right now no matter how daunting or unsettling it is."

Concern to Trust

Concern or worry can quickly paralyze the most capable and driven people. Similar to control, concern causes us to be preoccupied with situations and circumstances in our lives. However, concern never moves to action. It stays in the preoccupation phase. Have you found yourself thinking about that argument with a spouse or coworker again and again? Or worrying about your son or daughter because you feel helpless to help them?

Concern can be a killer to our momentum or productivity when it stays concern. Concern is an emotion that destabilizes actions rather than energizes them. Trust, on the other hand, energizes actions and helps us take the action required for the moment.

Maybe you can't get your child out of the situation they are in, but you can buy them a meal and listen to their plight empathetically, trusting that the situation will work itself out but taking the action that you are able to. Maybe you can't change the way your boss or spouse acts, but you can trust that if you take the right actions you can let go of the concern about what you can't control.

Trust mobilizes and concern paralyzes. Whatever it looks like for you, how can you make sure to not live in toxic concern but motivating trust? As we said before, trust always.

Wisdom: Critical Decisions in the Fog

I can't emphasize enough the importance of wisdom and decision making in the fog. As we finish the third principle, hear me say that I truly believe this principle can make or break your journey in the fog. Don't just quickly glance over this chapter and acknowledge the thought. Go back through and read it again, and ask yourself how you're applying the Wisdom Principle to your life.

As a coach for leaders and organizations of all types, I find myself asking leaders what their strengths are. I consistently hear the answer: decision making. I hate to tell you this, but it's not true. Let me say that in a different way. Decision making is often a weakness of leaders when they think it's a strength. Leaders often make decisions based on their gut or their experience of what they've done before. This decision framework will only work for so long.

Most leaders don't have a plan or framework for

making decisions, so when they get in a fog, they get completely lost because the impulse decisions of the past won't carry them into the future. I especially saw this post-COVID with leaders because the rules of the game had totally changed. In our new reality, we have to use wisdom to make decisions. We don't want to succumb to indecision in our lack of clarity and confusion.

I believe that's why Scripture talks so much about the nature of decision making and getting wisdom.

I challenge you to choose. Choose to engage. Choose to trust. Choose to embrace the paradox. Choose to impact others. We can make these choices and stay aware of the obstacles that get in our way. In the fog you can treasure wisdom, and even on your darkest days, you have the ability to choose.

Implementation Questions

In the Wisdom Principle we look at the challenge of making decisions as we drive through the fog. These choices are crucial, especially in dealing with adversity and in overcoming obstacles.

1. What do you like about how you deal with adversity and what do you wish you did better?
2. If adversity reveals character, what have you learned about yourself?
3. What choices can you make to deal wisely with adversity?
4. Which of the obstacles of complexity, control, complacency, and concern are most prevalent in your life? What choices can you make to deal with them?

Chapter 4
The Collaboration Principle

RECOMMENDED LISTENING AS YOU DRIVE:
Find Your People by Drew Holcomb and the Neighbors
This is How We Move by The Revivalists

Traveling With Others in the Fog

Not everyone loves me.
That is one of my biggest take-aways in driving through the fog. It's not that people become enemies or don't like you; it's that many people become indifferent when you no longer have anything to add to their lives. Or, in some cases, they are uncomfortable with your fog. They don't feel like they have anything to contribute or, frankly, they don't have time or energy to engage with you. I'm not trying to be cynical or negative toward people, but I

have learned the great opportunity in the fog is to find your people.

As much as people are crucial while driving through the fog, figuring out whom to connect with and how to engage with them is a challenge. It's no wonder that some people attempt to move forward alone. In my personal experience and in coaching others, I've found a lot of times people don't know how to engage with others anymore. That was my story. Having been a pastor, having been married, and then all of a sudden, I'm on my own. The loneliness was disorienting and deafening. I had really good friends that were seemingly avoiding me, not because they didn't care, but because it was so awkward for them.

As you might remember, I needed LASIK surgery to be able to see clearly. As I got older, I still needed "cheaters." I need to read, right? Unfortunately, surgery can't fix everything. I have my readers (or cheaters) with me all the time because I can see clearly unless I need to see something up close. If it's not size 20 font, I will have a hard time reading without help. In public presentations I can print out my notes and if I'm not careful it is a blurry mess. It's terrifying.

Similarly, we need help moving forward. Take those words in. We need help to read what we are seeing up ahead. People are needed to engage with in a new and deeper way. But it's hard to figure out what that looks like. How do we engage others to travel with us through the fog? It can be a challenge. It's very humbling when you're driving through fog because you can't see. People ask you questions: Where are you going? What are you doing? How are you, really? And you don't have the answers. Sometimes it can feel like everyone else is driving in clear weather. How do you talk, how do you communicate, how do you actually have conversations with people when you're driving through the fog?

My friend Roger is one of those amazing visionary leaders. He has led a successful software company and then became a pastor of a healthy, growing church. Futuristic sight has always come naturally to him. It's a God-given gift for him to look ahead. For Roger, plans and strategies flowed out of a vision for what the future could hold for himself and for the organization. Until it didn't.

Over the course of three years, Roger experienced two personal setbacks: a global pandemic and a city-wide culture conflict that created all kinds of interpersonal conflict. He described it as "the perfect storm." As he attempted to drive through the fog, he connected with me over a cup of coffee. He talked, and talked, and talked, rambling on and on about himself. I didn't blame him. I've been there before. And he wasn't ready to engage differently. Not yet. He wasn't prepared to collaborate. Collaboration is one of those words that everyone loves and yet very few people know how to do it. To collaborate is to work with someone to produce or create something. In this case, moving forward through the fog with others is a cooperative, relational experience. It requires a focus on each other and a path out of the fog, not just a focus on ourselves. For me personally, I learned to stop going on and on about myself and to focus on others. What this focus required was a whole new set of skills to relate and powerfully collaborate with people.

The Power of Curiosity

For many people, the ability to stop focusing on themselves as they drive through the fog seems impossible. After all, they can't see. Things are not what they were or what we expect them to be. Emotions become hard to deal with. But emotions do not give us the right to not take actions. For my friend Roger, his emotions of fear and anger dictated his narrative and then his actions. When our actions are under the authority of our feelings, we have lost the ability to lead ourselves forward. Engaging with our emotions but choosing a different behavior allows us to engage with others.

One important skill set that helps us choose to collaborate is found in cultivating curiosity.

At this very moment, I am sitting in my office at our home, and my dog has pushed his way into the room. Our dog is a beagle, and we love him. He is a part of our family, but we would never buy a beagle again or rescue a beagle, which is what we did in this case. I don't know if you know anything about beagles, but they have one love language and it is food. He will eat, anything and everything. I believe he would eat himself to death. Literally. When we have people over, it's embarrassing because he'll take food out of people's hands, right off their plates.

Our friends think it's really funny but we don't.

His name is Javy Baez Zehr, and he is named after the former Chicago Cubs infielder, Javy Baez, who was flamboyant and fun to watch. Javy, the baseball player, had the nickname El Mago, which is Spanish for "the magician." Our Javy is referred to as El Loco.

One thing that makes our Javy lovable is that he's super energetic and curious. He's curious about everything. He greets everyone with physical affection and asks with his body language, "Do you have anything I can eat?" Every morning we take an hour walk together, and his curiosity will be on full display. We'll be walking and suddenly he'll be eating something, and I will have no idea what it is. It's disgusting. He's just super, super curious. Maybe too curious.

Sometimes we refrain from being curious because we think we're going to be like Javy. We're going to be annoying, we're going to be finding all kinds of things and potentially bothering others. In reality, curiosity is one of the greatest character traits we could have. It's hard to not feel loved when someone is genuinely curious about us.

What does it take to be appropriately, genuinely curious?

One of the turning points in my drive through the fog was when I went through formal training to become an executive coach. For the past twenty years, I have been a consultant and a coach. They are very different from each other. Consultants give their expertise. They tell people what they should do. Coaches ask questions to help people process what is happening, leading to defining action. Asking the right questions can help us collaborate and not just act on our emotions. It's the art of choosing action.

The power of curiosity comes in the skill of asking questions, and when answers come, to clarify and to keep asking. These questions are best when they are open-ended, beginning with what or how. The goal is to learn and to work together in order to move forward. When I learned how to ask questions, it cultivated curiosity, and I began to get traction on the road through fog. Collaboration brings hope on the path forward, and curiosity gets it all started.

It's really about having dialogue instead of monologue.

The skills weren't overly complicated. Ask questions, really engage with people by asking, not telling, not directing, but by including. This is where collaboration comes in. Collaboration doesn't come from me telling you what to do. It comes from me asking and pulling things out of you. Asking questions is where you cultivate curiosity, where you strive to become an expert at collaborating.

You ask questions, and when someone gives you an answer, you ask a follow up question and then you keep asking questions. This is done until you reach a place where you're able to contribute yourself, and that's what I learned when you're going through the fog. You have to engage with people by being curious and asking questions. Don't just blurt out what's going on or what they should do. It may sound simple, but think before you speak and make sure it's not all about you.

Much has been said and written on the power of asking questions. When unwanted change puts us in a fog, we tend to stop listening and begin to panic. Cultivating the power of curiosity gives us an avenue to collaborate.

The one thing that I've been asked to do more than anything else in the last few years is train people in how to ask questions and how to coach people versus command people. Effective communication has moved away from authoritative, demanding types of interaction. Now things are much more collaborative. The most effective way to collaborate is to engage people by asking questions. You get everybody else's thoughts before you share yours. I found when you're driving through the fog, curiosity is a crucial skill set.

The Power of Listening

Who do you listen to? Let's say you have a question regarding a possible health situation. You have certain symptoms, and they are not going away. What do you do? You might reach out to your good friend Google and ask a question. As you sit at your computer, there is no shortage of answers that come flying at you. After ten minutes of reading, you have come to the conclusion that your life may be ending, and it may be ending soon. It's right there on the internet, so it must be true.

Everyone has an opinion, a thought, some advice, a criticism, and seemingly many feel the need to express it. Especially to those who are driving in the fog. Sometimes the difference between getting lost and finding our way forward is in who we listen to, and how we do it.

I've had friends get even more lost in the fog because of who they choose to listen to. Others experience a deep freedom because of the voices they allow into their lives.

A neighbor of mine named Bob has an extremely obedient dog. Bob walks his dog around the neighborhood without a leash. None needed. The dog is named Wrigley, after Wrigley Field, the home of the Chicago Cubs. One day I asked Bob how it is that Wrigley can be walked without a leash. Bob, being a bit of a show-off, decided to show me all the ways that Wrigley obeys. It was a bit annoying, especially since my dog is the poster-child for non-compliant disobedience, but Wrigley was amazing. It all came to a head when Bob said to me, "go ahead, call him. Tell him to come to you." I was about 15 feet away and I got down low, made eye contact with Wrigley, and said, "Wrigley, come here boy. Come here, Wrigley." Nothing. Not a twitch. Bob just starts walking away and with his back turned to both me and Wrigley, says, "Come." Wrigley shuffles up to his master. As a Cubs fan, I have been unsuccessfully telling things to move at Wrigley for most of my life, so there's nothing new about that.

But Wrigley didn't just listen for his name; he listened to a particular voice.

When we can't see where we are going, it is really important that our hearing is maximized. We can collaborate fully when we listen to the right voices around us. The Collaboration Principle is dependent on us listening to those who will help us move forward. In my own experience, some voices are best left unheard. I have found myself avoiding some people who bring fear and an ever-rising level of worry. There is enough anxiety in the fog without other voices yelling at us to not crash. Sometimes, well-meaning people make things worse by either describing the fog at an intense level or just bringing their own fear to the situation. One great question to ask ourselves is, "Do the people I am listening to bring anxiety or hope to my situation?" I want honesty, which is not always positive, but without the extra anxiety. I need encouragement and the reassurance that I am not alone. Collaboration requires choosing to whom we will and will not listen.

One day Jesus was in a bit of an argument with religious leaders. They were struggling with the fact that he was helping blind people see. In many ways, the leaders were blinded in the sense that they were unable to recognize who Jesus was and what he was doing. Jesus talked a bit about spiritual blindness, and he begins to use a metaphor to explain who he is and how people can actually respond to him. He describes himself as a shepherd, a good shepherd.

He says, "the shepherd speaks, and the sheep listen to his voice. He calls them by name and leads them out. When he has brought out all his own, he goes on ahead of them, and his sheep follow him because they know his voice." (John 10:26-30)

The greatest opportunity to collaborate is to learn to hear the voice of Jesus in the midst of the fog. It is the voice of peace and love in the midst of a myriad of other anxiety-filled voices.

I believe how closely we listen to his voice is a key indicator to how we navigate the fog.

The Power of Asking for Help

It was December 31, 1988, and it was one of the wildest experiences I have ever had. Even though it was a long time ago, I still remember it vividly. My friend Lance and I decided to go see our Chicago Bears play the Philadelphia Eagles in what is now referred to as the Fog Bowl. Meteorologists said that the fog was so thick at Soldier Field that it was like having clouds in the stadium. Cold air over Lake Michigan was blown by a breeze of warm air on the lakefront in Chicago, causing a complete lack of visibility over the field. As we watched, a haze came over the field and literally we no longer could see any of the players. We had no idea what was going on. Every once in a while we would see a player's arm or their legs running, and the fans would cheer loudly—for no reason. On the field, players had a bit of visibility, and up above in the sky boxes, people could somewhat see the action on the field. I don't know how it happened, but Lance got the attention of someone in one of the sky boxes, and they started giving each other hand signals. The man would gesture as to whether it was a running play or a passing play and what the results were. Occasionally, the announcer would tell us what happened on the field, but for the most part we were lost except for the communication of our new friend. It was the greatest game I never saw.

Sometimes in the midst of the fog, help comes from an unexpected source. When we are in the fog, we can't see anything, but somebody else can often see more than we can. We just need to ask. Pride is such a huge issue for people, especially when they need help the most. Many of us have a hard time asking for help. It requires courage and skill. It requires honest reflection and understanding of our limitations. The remedy, humility, is one of the greatest character traits in collaborating properly with people when you're driving through the fog. We must overcome pride. Pride tells us we can do it all on our own. That's one of the most dangerous lies we can believe. The power of asking for help can't be overstated or underemphasized.

Driving in traffic can induce a wide range of emotions, most of them not positive. I can go from calm to freaked out in a matter of seconds. One day I was on my way to see a client when the Chicago traffic bit me. We started crawling along for no apparent reason, and I realized I was going to be late. Nothing worse than being late. Calm one minute, antsy beyond belief the next. I was at a standstill in the right lane when suddenly, a car came flying up behind me on the shoulder of the road, going at least 60 miles per hour. Calm to antsy to extremely angry! Who did this driver think he was? He thought he was better than everyone else! How arrogant! The rules were for everyone but him! I was seething. I wanted a police car to be up ahead and pull him over so I could laugh as I crawled past him.

A few minutes later, I reached my exit and I quickly drove toward my client, knowing that I was late. As I hurried, I drove through a neighborhood and saw people, kids, walking on the sidewalks. I looked in the rear-view mirror and there were flashing lights of the police officer pulling me over. Where was he a few minutes ago on the highway? Turns out I was speeding in a school zone. As I sat in my car, fuming, I looked to my left and saw two moms looking directly at me with their arms crossed. One of them yelled something. Something to the effect of, "Who does he think he is? He thinks he's better than everyone else! How arrogant! The rules are for everyone but him!"

In that moment, I realized that in my anger at someone else's arrogance I had done the same thing. Who did I think I was? Certainly better than the other person. Truthfully, I was the same. The temptation when you can't see where you are going is to think that self-sufficiency is the goal and that there is no need to ask for help. Nothing could be further from the truth. Collaborating with others requires overcoming pride and realizing that we cannot see without the help of others.

As Jesus talks with the religious leaders about sight and about his followers hearing his voice, he makes a powerful statement to them about their own inability to collaborate with God or with others. He says, "the blind will see and those who see will become blind." Some Pharisees who were with him heard him say this and asked, "What? Are we blind too?" Jesus said, "If you were blind, you would not be guilty of sin; but now that you claim you can see, your guilt remains."

How will the blind see? Because they are humble and ask for help. They collaborate. How are those who think they can see blind? Because they believe they can see all on their own. They live closed rather than collaborative.

In your fog, will you collaborate? We all can cultivate curiosity, harness the power of listening, and overcome pride to ask for help.

It's okay to not have all the answers or not be able to fully see what's up ahead. That's why we have each other.

Implementation Questions

The Collaboration Principle has us learning a whole new set of skills to work with people to move through the fog.

1. In what areas are you struggling to work together with others?
2. What could you do to cultivate curiosity as part of your character?
3. Who do you consciously listen to for wisdom, empathy, and strength as you navigate through fog?
4. How good are you at asking for help?
5. What could you do to overcome pride?

"Every day you either get better or you get worse. You never stay the same."[1]

— Bo Schembechler

Chapter 5
The Intentionality Principle

RECOMMENDED LISTENING AS YOU DRIVE:
How do you feel by The Maine
Alive by NEEDTOBREATHE

Impact Depends on Intentionality

Do you remember the first time you drove in fog? Maybe you were taught about fog in drivers ed. I sure don't remember being given advice or it even being mentioned. As a driver, you may have seen fog rolling in and admired how beautiful it looked. Cloud-like haze in motion can truly be mesmerizing. But then as you drove into the fog, you realized that what was clear in front of you a minute ago is no longer visible. We recognize our limitations when our visibility is depleted. What happened to what I was looking at? Doubt creeps in, and we can feel an intense pressure to instantly do something to improve our sight. Perhaps you, like many who are new to driving in fog, decided to give the situation more light. After all, light gives sight. Illumination brings clarity. So you turned on your high beams. At once your sight was changed, but it was not what you hoped for or needed. The high beams shone directly into the precipitation causing the fog, which reflected the bright light back to you. The dangerous result was a wall of glare, which made it even more difficult for you to see the road. Suddenly, driving in the fog became more intense, and the pressure became almost unbearable.

In any personal or leadership fog that we face, there comes a point where the intensity and the pressure threatens to get the best of us. Instead of being able to see more, we find ourselves stuck with less vision than ever.

Experientially, I have found that the phrase "two steps forward, three steps back" is a very real concept.

What can we do when the intensity ramps up and the pressure threatens to take us off course?

The temptation is to keep trying to turn the lights on brighter. We work harder, we hustle more, and we turn up our control. But this just blinds us more. Instead of turning on the brights, we need to slow down and observe our surroundings. Sometimes that requires taking a step back. There is a need to be

The Intentionality Principle

intentional in how we move forward and in what we pursue. That brings us to the Intentionality Principle, where we realize that we need to personally grow as we move through the fog.

There were 75 of us crammed into an Indianapolis hotel banquet room. Our speaker for the day had flown in from California and I, for one, was eager and ready to learn. I had recently become a leader with numerous responsibilities and multiple people reporting to me. This level of leadership was new to me, and even though it was exciting, it was also a little frightening. I had no idea what I was doing or where we were going. It was an exhilarating fog, but I couldn't see where to go.

Our speaker was introduced, and as the applause died down, he looked out at the audience. His first words have stuck with me for the past thirty years. He said, "How many of you have a plan for how you are going to grow your organization?" Every person raised their hand. Even the people who were lying. As the hands went down, he asked a follow-up question: "How many of you have a plan to grow yourself?" No hands went up. Not a single one. He said, "How are you going to do the one when you don't do the other? How can you intentionally grow your responsibilities if you don't intentionally grow yourself?"

Everyone in the room gave an audible, "Hhhmmm," and wrote it down.

As for me, the moment kicked off a journey toward intentional growth, and with it an asset of behaviors and a narrative that is invaluable to anyone driving through fog.

How intentional are you in your own growth, in your own development? The answer to the question is the difference maker in dealing with the intensity and the high beam glare of moving forward when you cannot see where you are going.

We can't impact others unless we are intentional about growing ourselves.

I've previously talked about growth plans and how we can make sure we are investing in ourselves. But for this principle I'm going to take what some may think is a surprising turn. For this I'm going to take the lead from Jesus, who I believe is the best example of intentional growth.

Intentionality Modeled by Jesus

History tells us that on the night that Jesus was betrayed, he took off his coat, wrapped a towel around his waist, put water in a basin, and moved one by one to each of his followers. His purpose? Cleanliness. Sandals and dirt roads are not a good mix for personal hygiene. Culturally, the washing of feet was either done by people themselves as they walked into a house, or servants washed their feet for them. The menial task was certainly not done by one whom others considered to be their master or rabbi. But Jesus did it. You may be familiar with the story of how Jesus washed his followers' feet and told them to do the same for others. Often this story is told as an example of serving others, and it is. But the process and outcome of this ceremonial foot washing is about much more than service. It is an intentional movement toward intimacy.

There are certain character traits necessary for a person to humble themselves enough to serve at this level. Traits that are acquired with a purposeful pursuit. It's a maturity developed with the intent of putting other people ahead of oneself, resulting in a depth of relationship. It requires a person to have nothing to prove, nothing to lose, and nothing to hide.

As Jesus wrapped the towel around his waist, he had nothing to prove. He could get down on his knees and get dirty because he knew who he was. He knew that he was the son of God, and when you know who you are, you don't have to prove anything to anybody. No need to spin, no need to look good. He had nothing to prove.

Having to prove ourselves takes up so much time and energy.

Jesus also had nothing to hide. Everything had been given under his authority and everything would become known. He could let his whole life be seen. He had nothing to hide.

Jesus also had nothing to lose. He knew that what

you gain in this world, you lose, and what you give away in this life comes back to us for eternity. He had nothing to lose.

This is the challenge of the intentionally lived life. Driving through fog, unable to see what is up ahead, brings great opportunity to live the intimate life—where you have nothing to prove, nothing to hide, and nothing to lose.

Think of it this way. If you have nothing to prove, you can be totally authentic with each other. No spin, no need to look good, because you know who you are.

Nothing to hide is a little different. It requires more than authenticity; it requires transparency. Your feelings, your insecurities, your weaknesses—let them be seen by each other and live with nothing to hide.

Even as Jesus lived with nothing to lose, he showed total vulnerability giving his life for others. Some haze-filled situations leave us wanting to hold onto what we have–to hold back–to not lose and to not give ourselves away.

This is the intentional life that Jesus modeled.

Intentionality Leads to Intimacy

The story of Jesus washing his disciples feet is found in John 13 of the Bible. At the end of this description, Jesus' friend John records Jesus saying, "A new

The Intentionality Principle

command I give you, love one another. The way that I have loved you—that is the way to love each other." On the way to the cross, Jesus had nothing to prove, nothing to lose, and nothing to hide.

Driving through fog has us trying to prove ourselves, trying to make sure we are seen a certain way—to not lose, hiding our true selves because we really don't know what is out there.

Let me ask you:

What will you give your life for? Even if it is unknown? When you are in the fog, you have a choice: live for yourself or for others. Will you trust God or try to prove yourself, try to win, try to hide what really goes on?

I want to give my life to being in loving relationships with God and with others. To go through the fog with others, serving them, loving them.

If I have nothing to PROVE → AUTHENTIC, there is no spin. There's no attempt to look good.

If I have nothing to HIDE → TRANSPARENT, there is no covering—all is laid bare.

If I have nothing to LOSE → VULNERABLE, there is a possibility of pain—you have the knowledge to hurt me.

When I am intentionally pursuing these three

components in my relationship with God and others, I find → INTIMACY. I will give my life to be used by God through meaningful connection with God and people.

Intimacy is at the core of our longings, decisions, and desires. Intimacy is what we need to thrive as humans. And intimacy doesn't happen by accident. It requires intentionality, and it requires a plan for growth. Thinking through the three lenses of nothing to prove, nothing to hide, and nothing to lose will help us develop an intentional plan for growth and intimacy.

Nothing to prove. When you have nothing to prove, it leads to authenticity. Authenticity is invaluable to the leader who seeks to build trust and gain influence. In much of leadership culture, we spend so much time proving and positioning ourselves. Allow me to encourage you by saying you have nothing to prove. Your authentic self is the self the world needs even when you are driving through the fog. When you intentionally don't try to look good and instead be who you are, you experience a deep freedom.

Where are you trying to prove yourself in your life? Who are you trying to prove yourself to? A coworker, a boss, a friend, a spouse? What would it look like for you to stop proving and instead live authentically?

Nothing to hide. When you have nothing to hide, it leads to transparency. Transparency is a gift in our world which is so full of fashioning and trying to make ourselves look better. Transparency is fear-inducing for many of us. What will people do when they see us for who we really are? We can't control other people's actions, but we can control our transparency. Allowing people to see what's happening in our lives, especially during times of crises, allows us to be seen and known and belong.

What are you trying to hide in your life? What would it look like to be transparent and let go of the weight of your secrets? We often don't realize the weight of our burdens until we stop holding them. In order to live intentionally and live intimately, transparency is required.

Nothing to lose. When you have nothing to lose, it leads to vulnerability. As discussed previously, many of us live with a scarcity mindset. We worry about what we will accumulate, what we will lose, and how we will survive even though we live in abundance. The only way to truly gain abundance is to have an abundance mindset no matter what your circumstances are. You truly have nothing to lose. There is always a possibility of pain in life and relationships. Accepting pain and knowing you'll be okay allows you to truly live life.

What are you worried about losing? An item, a platform, a reputation? What we worry about losing is usually a key indicator of what we love the most.

How can you move toward trust, abundance, and intentionally letting go for the sake of intimacy?

The goal of intentionality isn't just to become a better person. It's to foster intimacy with God, yourself, and others. Intimacy helps clear the fog in our lives more than almost anything else. It creates clarity, connection, and freedom—some of the things we long for most when we are driving through fog.

Intimacy doesn't happen by accident, and if you prioritize intimacy in the fog, you'll achieve the growth you long for.

You Can't Give What You Don't Have

The sun was too much for me. I had spent the better part of a week in Daytona with a large group of young people. We were on the beach every day, and after a while, it felt like I was baking. Too many people and too much heat. Leaving my backpack with my friends on the beach, I decided to take a walk by myself. After a bit, I found a Ron Jon surf shop with all sorts of surf gear and beach apparel. The store was crowded with others looking to escape the heat. Suddenly, a very loud group of young boys walked in. Three of them looked to be about twelve years old with one younger brother tagging along, who looked to be about nine. That youngest boy made the most noise. He would pick up an item and scream to the others about how awesome everything was. Suddenly he grabbed a shirt off the rack and shoved it into the older boys' faces. "This is the best shirt ever! I have my own money, and I am going to buy this." I was to the side, watching the older boys try to ignore the loud antics of their younger friend. The young one made his way over to the cashier and started pulling out wads of one-dollar bills along with loose change that ran all over the counter. The young woman behind the counter rolled her eyes as she gathered up the money. Finally, she looked up at him and said, "You are $3.52 short."

At this point the other boys kick in and start poking fun at the nine-year-old. "Oh, mister big shot has his own money! You can't even buy this shirt." As they laughed, I found myself doing something that I have never done before. I could not help myself. Stepping out from the other side of the cashier, I said, "Excuse me, $3.52? Here, let me take care of that." And I reached back for my wallet—which I had left in my backpack down at the beach. As it became apparent that I had no money, the young boy went from looking at me like I was his savior to seeing me as the devil himself.

No matter how much you want to care about others or to make an impact with your life, you cannot give away what you don't have. If we are not intentional in how we grow both in our habits and in our ability to develop deep, intimate relationships, we will find ourselves reaching into our pockets with great intent, only to find that they are empty. You can't give away what you don't have. Intentionality requires a commitment to obtaining habits and traits that can be given for a greater impact than we can ever imagine. Intentionality leads to intimacy which leads to impact.

Implementation Questions

In the Intentionality Principle we focus on overcoming the pressure of driving through the fog by making sure that we deliberately grow.

1. What would it look like for you to have a plan for how you grow yourself?
2. What kind of impact do you want to have on others?
3. Intimacy comes from having nothing to prove, nothing to hide, and nothing to lose. How can you grow in being authentic, transparent, and vulnerable?
4. Having an impact on others requires us to give away what we have been given. What do you have that you can give away to others?

Chapter 6
The Hope Principle

RECOMMENDED LISTENING AS YOU DRIVE:
Better Days by One Republic
If Your Light Goes Out by The Maine

Hope in the Pain

Hope can trick you, and it leaves you different. I included hope as the final principle not because I want to bake you cookies and leave you a sugary Disney princess end.

Hope is the final principle for driving through the fog because it's absolutely essential and critically endangered in our world.

When I talk about hope, I'm not talking about unrealistic expectations that everything will be okay. I'm talking about a confident expectation and desire for something good in the future.

I would argue when you look at life realistically, you have hope.

For people whose everyday life is a fog, hope can seem impossible and improbable. Hope is missing from our world, and while it's contagious, there are hope deserts where it is in short supply. Whole communities in our world find hope a scarcer resource than water.

Ephesians 1:18 says, "I pray that the eyes of your heart may be enlightened in order that you may know the hope to which he has called you."

God has called us to hope. And the people who make the biggest impact on others are people of hope.

1 Corinthians 13:13 says, "And now these three remain: faith, hope and love."

Faith and love get a lot of air time. Paul does go on to say the greatest of those three things is love. But I'm convinced if hope is one of three things that remains, it deserves a whole lot more attention.

But here's the twist with hope. The price of getting to hope is not fun.

Trail Ridge Road holds the distinction of being the highest paved highway in the United States. It stretches from Estes Park to Grand Lake through the amazing Rocky Mountain National Park in beautiful Colorado. The altitude of this route reaches more than 12,000 feet above the tree line for approximately eleven miles. It is breathtaking both in its

The Hope Principle

visual beauty and in its oxygen-deprived height. My wife, Judy, and I were driving this road one October, only a few weeks before the weather would require the road to be shut down. We began our drive with—you guessed it—a lot of fog. We drove slowly and with complete focus. Judy white-knuckled the passenger side door as she looked into the haze. We caught glimpses of trees along the side of the road, but the beauty of the terrain was lost as we slowly moved forward. It is pretty common to lose the beauty of your surroundings when you are in survival mode. It happens in every kind of fog.

As we climbed up, up, and hopefully not away, we noticed something up ahead. Slowly, our vision changed. We could see more. It started with the skyline forming. Blue sky, a few amazing cloud formations. We were starting to see what was ahead! We could make out the trees and some rock structures with breath-taking cliffs in the distance. Just when we started to relax and enjoy—just when we thought we were clear of whatever danger the fog had brought—we were able to look down. We wish we hadn't looked down. We could see more, and we realized that we were only a couple of feet away from the edge. One wrong turn, one careless mistake, and it would be a disaster.

Hope is a funny thing. Hope tricks us. Just when you start to see clearly and you begin to think you are coming out of it, you realize that what has been around you all along is not what you want to see. Hope begins, and then we look down. What we see shapes our pursuits.

Where do you go when hope runs out? Hope is arguably one of the components of life that is missing the most. In many cases, it is fleeting, and when we look down, we aren't really sure how to get it back. On a personal note, I have made some of my biggest mistakes pursuing hope. And I have seen others fail in the same way. When hope runs out, we tend to run away. The mindset becomes one of fixing situations. I'm in the fog, let me fix it by clearing the fog away as quickly as possible.

- My friend Joe lost his marriage, so he quickly got mad and looked for a new wife.
- Chris is a pastor whose church has changed drastically over the pandemic and now the future is uncertain. What does Chris do? Look for a new one.
- Brian (yes, that's me) lost relationships that meant so much to him. Rather than grieve, I tried to accumulate replacement friends as quickly as possible.

Well, it doesn't quite work because no matter where you are, there you are. You take yourself with you. And if you were deficient of hope before the loss, then you will continue to be.

The Hope Principle consists of three crucial factors. In order to find and keep hope, there is a need to grieve, a need to grow, and a need to embrace the process.

A Need to Grieve

Grief is not fun. I don't know anyone who likes to grieve or looks forward to grief. Instead of grieving, we often look for a quick and clear solution. The problem is that there is a lot of false hope out there. Especially if you are driving through fog. Anytime the fog lifts, the temptation is to jump to a conclusion that everything is okay, right now! It's not. We need to grieve.

In the summer of my senior year of college, my friend Ross committed suicide. No one saw it coming. My school was 220 miles from home, and I remember the numbness I felt on the drive home and the hopelessness I felt on the way back. It was my first experience with suicide but certainly not my last. Since then I have been to countless services of both friends and friends of friends who have taken their own lives in a display of bleak depression. It did start me on a journey of trying to deal with grief and loss. When hope is fleeting, the deterioration of life seems to follow.

In his book entitled, *A Grace Disguised*, author Jerry Sittser describes a horrific scene that threatened all hope for both him and members of his family. In an instant, a tragic car accident claimed three generations of his family: his mother, his wife, and his young daughter. That kind of loss is hard to fathom and yet we all experience loss. Where do you go when the hope runs out?

As Sittser suffered this loss of loved ones, he came to a painful realization. It was a realization of grief that was tied to moving forward. He writes, "Living means changing, and change requires that we lose one thing before we gain something else." The grieving of loss is essential to moving forward. Without grief and the change that loss brings, hope can trick us. We believe we can suddenly see where we are going, only to find that the edge of the cliff is right there.

In his grief process, Sittser gives a clear direction for us to take.

He says, "The quickest way for anyone to reach the sun and the light of day is not to run west, chasing after the setting sun, but to head east, plunging into the darkness until one comes to the sunrise."

Moving into the darkness instead of chasing the sun seems counter-intuitive, but eventually the light comes. In the deepest fog of my life, I found that refusing to run away from loss was the path to the light, both with God and with the situations that brought the fog. You see, grief is actually a great companion.

A last lesson that I learned from Jerry Sittser is this: "Loss can also make us more. In the darkness we can still find the light. In death we can also find life. It depends on the choices we make. Though these choices are difficult and rarely made in haste or with ease, we can nevertheless make them."[1]

Grief can make us more. In my experience, your soul becomes thicker. What was thin before, becomes larger, more impactful, more substantial. Where there was empathy in a small dose, for me now, it is large. Where love was conditional, it now gives grace and mercy. In many of the traits of love, grief brings more, and with it, hope.

A Need to Grow

A while back, Judy and I and some friends went to the House of Blues in Chicago to see pop artist Andy Grammer. He's awesome. He is so positive, so authentic and raw, so deeply spiritual. In many ways, he is Christ-like, but he is not a professing Christian.

When we were at his sold-out concert, he paused between songs and said to the audience, "Is there anyone here who has gone through really hard situations in their life and come out of it changed? Anybody willing to share a hard thing in their life and how they are better for having gone through it?"

I thought, "Wow, I would never share that in front of a crowd of strangers at a concert."

But shockingly, three or four people raised their hands. The friends of a woman standing in front of us all pointed to her.

Andy told her, "Come on up."

The crew grabbed a stool for her to sit on next to Andy, and he asked her a couple of questions. She authentically talked about her pain. She described betrayal, both physical and emotional pain. It was raw. It was real.

Andy was curious about her pain and especially about how her pain had changed her. She shared how she was more empathetic to others, how she had compassion where she didn't before. She wouldn't wish her situation on anyone else, but she was better for having gone through her pain. The whole conversation took about five minutes, and I couldn't help but feel like I was experiencing church. At least how it is supposed to be.

Then Andy Grammer sent her off stage and sang a song. It's called "Wish you Pain." I encourage you to look up the lyrics for yourself and listen to it on your own.

He poetically describes how pain, in all its searing hurt, has the power to transform.[2]

When we love someone, we have to be able to let

them experience pain. Usually we think love protects us from pain, but love moves with us through the pain. It's certainly the hardest part of being a parent or a friend. When have you grown the most? Good times? Probably not.

Here is a great exercise: Trace the hard, painful times in your life. Maybe even the situation you are in now. What are you learning? How is it making you better? The paradox of the pain of the fog is that it moves us in the direction of growth if we let it.

And as Andy Grammer's song says, "It's hard to say, but I wish you pain."

Could it be that the path to hope runs directly through pain?

What does this have to do with hope?

When Andy Grammer asked the question, I could have raised my hand. I didn't, but I could have. When we are driving in fog, there is a need to learn and grow from pain. It is the path of hope.

A Need to Embrace the Hope Process

The need for patience is critical in what I call the hope process. The hope process is the movement through pain to hope. The process takes longer because we try to fight it rather than embrace it. It is the path of chasing the sunrise instead of the sunset.

Acquiring hope when you can't see where you are going is a journey that very few people want to take. It requires a process that is incredibly unappealing. It requires grief and growth, but more than that, it requires a personal change that one cannot come back from.

In Romans 5:2, we are told that Paul boasts in the glory of God, but then he says this:

> "Not only so, but we also glory in our sufferings, because we know that suffering produces perseverance; perseverance, character; and character, hope. And hope does not put us to shame, because God's love has been poured out into our hearts through the Holy Spirit, who has been given to us."

He describes a process that is both sequential and mandatory.

Suffering, and the difficulties and pain that come from it, produces perseverance.

Perseverance, the continued effort to do or achieve something despite difficulties, failure, or opposition, not looking down and giving up steadfastness, produces character.

Character, who you have become as you drive through the fog, leaves you with a never-ending, alert expectation called hope.

But here is the challenge: There is a need to embrace the process. Jumping from suffering to hope is not possible. My experience supports what this

Scriptural wisdom and logic says. When I begin to see hope and I look down to actually see where I am going, hope disappears. It's too quick. I haven't grieved. I haven't grown. But when I have persevered and have developed character through time, the next step is genuine, life-altering hope.

You want to live a life of hope? Here is the process. Embrace it. Live it. Teach it. Stop trying to jump from suffering to hope. The Hope Principle encourages us to grieve, grow, and hope. Allowing this to happen, even while we are still in the fog, will free us to live with hope.

Hope is a scarce resource because so many people want to skip over their pain. But hope can be abundant for you.

Implementation Questions

Hope is a confident expectation and desire for something great that is up ahead. The Hope Principle shows us the need to grieve, the need to grow, and the need to embrace the process.

1. Would you describe yourself as someone who lives with hope? What is missing to bring more hope into your life?
2. What part does grief play in your life?
3. How are you better from having gone through painful experiences?
4. How does the hope process play out in the fog that you have found yourself in?

Our Final Destination

Recommended Listening as You Drive:
Brighter Days by Blessing Offor

We started this journey with a story from Mark 8. I told you only half the story, and understanding the end of this story is key to understanding our final destination.

In Mark 8, a blind man is brought to Jesus by his friends. They ask Jesus to heal him from his blindness. We don't even know if the blind man believes that Jesus can heal him, but his friends do. And Jesus does the strangest thing. He spits on the blind man's eyes. Then Jesus touches him and asks him a simple yet life-altering question: "Can you see anything?"

The blind man responds, "I see people, but they look like trees."

Jesus laid his hands on his eyes again, and the

man opened his eyes. This time his sight was restored, and he saw everything clearly.

Notice Jesus chose to heal the man's sight in stages. In between the first and second stage, the man lived in a fog. I'm not sure why Jesus chose to touch him twice, but here is what I know for sure. Even though you may be in the fog now, there will be a day when your sight is restored and you see everything clearly. It may not happen in your timing or preferred method, and your sight may never be restored perfectly, but if you continue the journey with Jesus, I wholeheartedly believe you will see clearly.

The golf ball was down in the gully left of the fairway in thick grass about four feet below the surface of the green, dangerously close to marshlands commonly found in southern Florida. Three friends and I were on our annual golf trip, and we were just getting started. I grabbed a high lofted club and made my way down into the gully. It was not an easy shot. As I hit down on the ball and watched a high trajectory pitch make its way onto the green, I cried out in pain. The pain had come suddenly, shockingly, to the bottom half of my legs. As I looked down, both legs from knees to ankles were completely covered in ants. These were not normal ants. These were ants sent straight from hell!

My friends and I frantically wiped off all the

ants. It was one of the creepiest experiences I have ever had. Once the ants were off, we kept playing.

About two hours later, I found myself dragging. No energy, completely fatigued. I was still beating the other guys, but I was not doing good.

When we went back to the condo we were staying at, I was completely worn out. Before I crashed for the night, I looked down at my legs. Welts were everywhere. I mean everywhere! In the medicine cabinet, I found a tube of Neosporin, a topical antibiotic ointment used to treat minor skin injuries. I put it all over my legs and went to sleep.

Morning came and the welts were bigger and my energy worse. I put more of the topical cream onto my legs and gave it my best effort. We left to play golf, and I got through about half of the round before my fatigue gave way to sheer exhaustion. One of my friends called a local pharmacist to ask a couple of questions. After explaining the situation to him, my friend hands me the phone. The first words I hear are "Dude!" (it was nice to know my medical condition was in good hands) "How many welts do you have on your legs?" I looked down and started to count. After forty I stopped and told him that I had at least fifty different bites on my legs. "Dude," he said again. "Those are not regular ants, and those are not bites. Those are fire ants, and they have stung you with their poison!"

I was not familiar with fire ants. We don't have

them in Chicago. "Well," I said. "I have been putting Neosporin on them." He started laughing, I mean really laughing. "Neosporin? That's going to do nothing. You can't put cream on the outside of your legs and hope that it heals the poison that's on the inside!" He proceeded to tell me how to deal with the poison. "Take a needle or a pick of some kind and scrape open all of the welts. Then, go buy a tube of Preparation H. Spread the cream all over your legs."

This was too much for me. I said, "Dude! I thought that was for something else!" Preparation H is a medicinal cream that brings relief primarily if you have hemorrhoids!

As crazy as it sounded, I did exactly what he prescribed. I scraped open every welt. Nasty. Then taking the Preparation H, I spread it onto each welt. As the cream went into the welt, not onto the welt, a strange phenomenon took place. The welts began to ooze with a volcanic type of reaction as the poison slowly made its way out of my bloodstream. Evidently putting Preparation H on fire ant stings gets inside where the poison is and causes the poison to leave. It's an inside-out job.

I had been trying to solve my problem by adding a little something to the outside of my skin when in reality, healing had to come from the inside out.

Over the course of this book, we have looked at principles that become a way of life in dealing with the fact that we cannot see where we are going. Prin-

Our Final Destination

ciples that ground us, prepare us, and give us skills and priority to invest in people and to find meaning. More than anything, these principles carve a path forward whereby change occurs. They are not a topical cream to be placed on top of our everyday challenges. Instead, they shape our lives, preparing us for the life that Jesus promised when he described his purpose to bring life to its fullest. Driving through the fog, when done correctly, is an inside-out job, and we are forever changed.

In writing this book, I am inviting you to a new way of living, and I hope these principles change your life. From my own experience, I want to assure you there is another side of the fog. I want to assure you that you are not alone. I also want to remind you that there are not quick fixes, but there are principles we can embrace and live by. Building your foundation. Making priorities. Trusting wisdom. Choosing collaboration. Living intentionally. Embracing hope.

I want to journey with you to your final destination, whatever that might look like.

The Hawaiian Islands are some of the most beautiful places on earth. It is so gorgeous I believe God vacations in Hawaii. It took me almost ten years of saving up airline miles, but Judy and I were finally able to go to Maui. After a nearly nine-hour flight, the anticipation was almost unbearable.

The pilot's voice over the speakers told us we would land in twenty minutes, so Judy and I reached over to pull up the window shade so that we could look out. You guessed it, all we could see was fog. Heavy clouds with zero visibility. All the adrenalin that we had been feeling just kind of dissipated as we looked out at the haze. We knew we were moving forward, but we could see nothing. We would need to wait as we flew toward our destination.

We felt the change before we saw it. There was a drop, a noticeable drop, as the plane suddenly descended, and the fog disappeared right before our eyes. In its place: paradise.

Your fog may seem like it will last forever. And honestly, I can't tell you how long it will last or where you will end up. I'm not promising you paradise, but I am promising that the fog doesn't last forever. One day you will find yourself out of the fog. You will see clearly, and you will be better for it. You will make an impact on others because of it.

Here's to driving through the fog.

Acknowledgments

There are so many people whom I appreciate and want to thank. Connor Zehr and Bailey Long have been so encouraging in this project, and I am so proud to call you my son and daughter. You are so great!

I am also grateful for my parents, Dave and Jackie Zehr, who laid the foundation and always pointed me in the right direction.

There are many who over the years have driven with me through the fog. Some continue to live life with me. People like Lance Kammes, Kellie Kammes, Dan Glod, Carrie Glod, Ken Cook, Lori Cook, Kurt Menner, Lisa Menner, Vic Vance, and Kevin Olsen. I love you and appreciate you so much.

I am also grateful for the partnership and friendship of Bruce Hanson and Nick Plassman who reinforced and shared with me the value of Intentional Impact. Little did we know how much it was going to change us and make us unafraid of the fog.

Over the years Community Christian Church with Dave and Jon Ferguson (and others) has given so much leadership that impacted the priority of this book. Thank you for creating an environment that impacts so many.

I would be remiss to not acknowledge and thank the people at Streamline Books. From my initial conversation with Alex Demzcak and Will Severns, to the team that worked with me on this book I have been encouraged and affirmed. Thanks to Trevor Waite, Jacob Vangen, Sara Brunsvold, and others. Everyone has a story to tell, and as you say, "the world needs your book."

My greatest appreciation is for my wife, Judy, who walks with me in every season. Your support and push is a constant source of inspiration.

Lastly, I'm not sure how people live without Jesus. I am so glad I never have to.

About the Author

As a former Pastor and Entrepreneur, Brian Zehr has spent his entire adult life in the People Development business. As a Speaker, Leadership Consultant, and Executive Coach, Brian focuses on helping people move from point A–where they currently are–to point B–where they want to go. Brian's passion is to help leaders and organizations grow through inspiration, insight, and instruction. His desire is to see people understand, define, and shape their culture, resulting in lives of hope and confidence. Brian has two adult children and lives with his wife, Judy, in the Chicago suburbs.

www.drivingthroughfog.com

Notes

1. The Foundation Principle

1. Lencioni, Patrick M. "Make Your Values Mean Something." Harvard Business Review, January 30, 2023. https://hbr.org/2002/07/make-your-values-mean-something.
2. Ramsey, Dave. Essay. In *Entreleadership: 20 Years of Practical Business Wisdom from the Trenches*, 82. Nashville, TN: Howard Books, 2011.

3. The Wisdom Principle

1. Bandy, Thomas G. Essay. In *Spiritual Leadership: Why Leaders Lead and Who Seekers Follow*, 10–13. Nashville, TN: Abingdon Press, 2016.
2. Sanchez, Robert. "When Anthony Rizzo Was Diagnosed with Cancer, Jon Lester Threw Him a Lifeline." ESPN, September 28, 2016. https://www.espn.com/mlb/story/_/id/17659023/cancer-survivors-contenders-anthony-rizzo-jon-lester-bond-goes-deeper-cubs.
3. Herrington, Ryan. "The Story behind Masters Amateur Star Sam Bennett's Tattoo Is Inspiring and Heartbreaking." GolfDigest.com, April 7, 2023. https://www.golfdigest.com/story/masters-2023-sam-bennett-amateur-tattoo-mark-bennett.
4. "In Quotes: Apple's Steve Jobs." BBC News, October 6, 2011. https://www.bbc.com/news/world-us-canada-15195448.
5. Berry, Clayton. "Jesuit Philosopher Recounts Time with Mother Teresa." Catholic Education Resource Center. Accessed July 8, 2023. https://www.catholiceducation.org/en/faith-and-character/faith-and-character/jesuit-philosopher-recounts-time-with-mother-teresa.html.

6. *We bought a zoo.* DVD. United States: 20th Century Fox, 2011.

5. The Intentionality Principle

1. Schembechler, Bo, and John Bacon. *Bo's lasting lessons: The legendary coach teaches the timeless fundamentals of leadership.* New York, NY: Business Plus, 2008.

6. The Hope Principle

1. Sittser, Gerald L. A Grace Disguised: How the Soul Grows through Loss. Grand Rapids, MI: Zondervan, 2004.
2. Andy Grammer Concert. House of Blues. Chicago, IL US. September 24, 2019.

www.ingramcontent.com/pod-product-compliance
Lightning Source LLC
Chambersburg PA
CBHW070157100426
42743CB00013B/2942